RANDOM GUY

Erotica Short Stories

A collection of 15 taboos

Copyright © 2024 by Random Guy

All rights reserved. No part of this publication may be reproduced, stored or transmitted in any form or by any means, electronic, mechanical, photocopying, recording, scanning, or otherwise without written permission from the publisher. It is illegal to copy this book, post it to a website, or distribute it by any other means without permission.

This novel is entirely a work of fiction. The names, characters and incidents portrayed in it are the work of the author's imagination. Any resemblance to actual persons, living or dead, events or localities is entirely coincidental.

All the images are generated through AI, none of them are related to any real person...

First edition

This book was professionally typeset on Reedsy. Find out more at reedsy.com

Contents

Warning	1
Teacher Student	3
The Aunty Next Door	22
Professor OLIVIA	33
Next Door Boys	47
Mysterious Couple Next Door	58
Friends sister	74
Free Use Girl	82
The Gym Instructor	89
Friend's daughter	103
Nurse	116
Lesbian Friend	125
A Party Invitation	130
Met In Club	137
Aunt Ana	145
Experiments	156

Warning

18+ only

The Stories are just imaginations and all the images are generated by AI. None of them related to any living person.

EROTICA SHORT STORIES

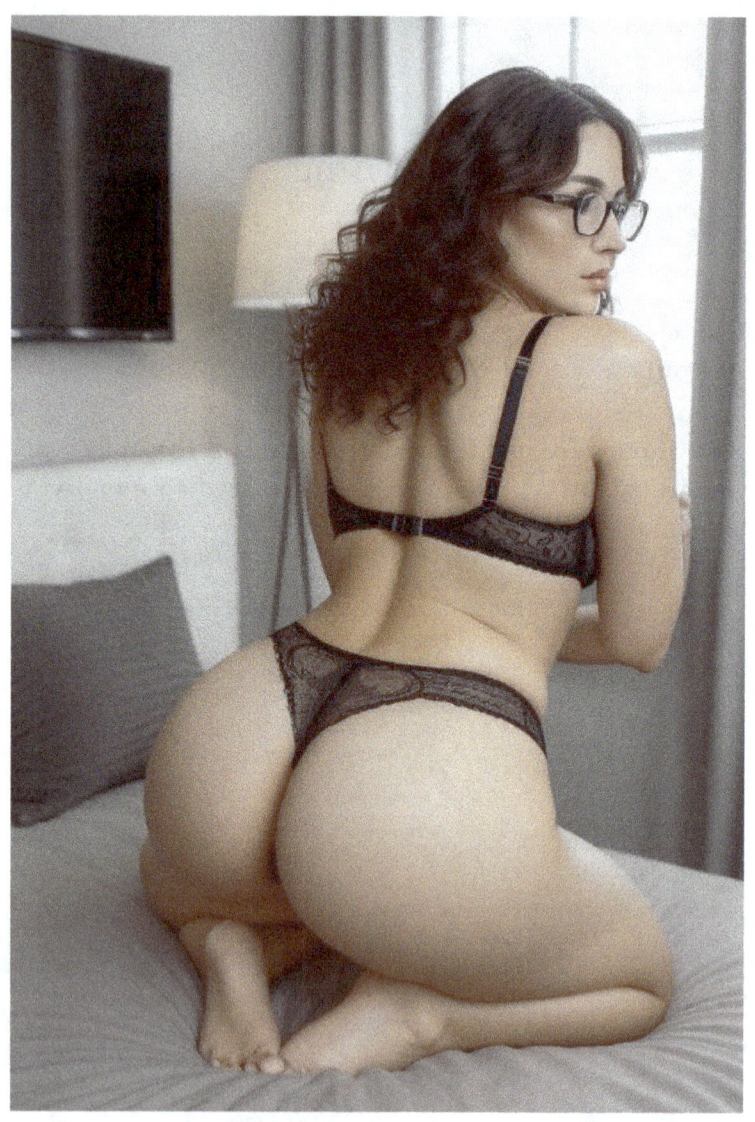

Teacher Student

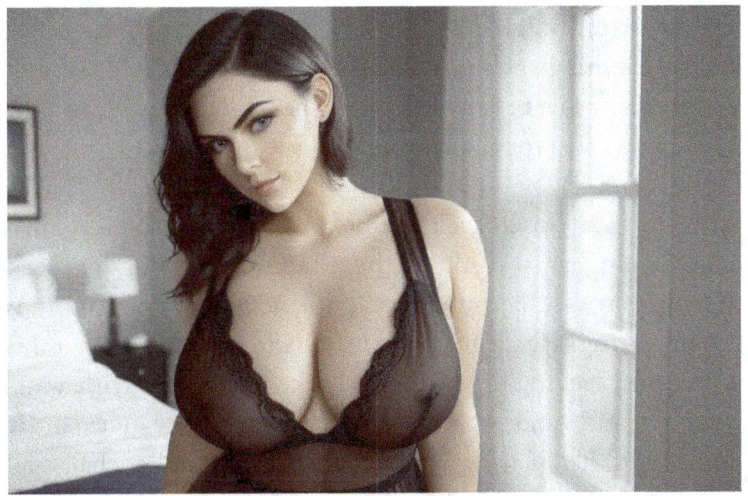

Mr. Jameson, a seasoned teacher in his early forties, had been harboring a secret craving for the young, supple body of his 19 years old student, Jenna. Jenna, a senior with raven hair and piercing blue eyes, had always had a certain allure that made her the center of attention in the classroom. Her tight skirts and low-cut tops did nothing to quell the raging desires that the male students, and even some of the teachers, felt for her. But it was Mr. Jameson who had the power to act on his impulses.

Jenna had been flirting with Mr. Jameson all semester, bending over his desk to give him a peek at her ample cleavage, and leaning against the chalkboard with her back arched, allowing her skirt to ride up and reveal the lacy tops of her stockings. He knew she was playing a game, and he was more than willing to play along. It was during one of these "innocent" exchanges that the opportunity presented itself. Jenna had come to his office hours, claiming she needed help with a particularly difficult assignment. The room was empty, the hallways quiet, and the setting was ripe for seduction.

Mr. Jameson closed the door behind her and leaned against it, watching as she sat in the chair in front of his desk. Her legs crossed and uncrossed, the gentle sway of her hips mesmerizing. He cleared his throat and approached her, his eyes never leaving her face. She looked up at him with a mix of anticipation and innocence that made his pulse quicken. He leaned over her, placing a hand on the armrest of her chair, and whispered in her ear, "I think I know what you really need help with, Jenna." Her eyes widened, and she bit her bottom lip, a silent invitation for him to continue.

He reached out and traced a finger along the neckline of her blouse, watching as her chest heaved with every shallow breath she took. He leaned closer, his breath warm against her neck, and whispered, "You've been driving me crazy all year, you know that?" Jenna's cheeks flushed, and she nodded, a small smile playing on her lips. Mr. Jameson took it as an affirmation of his suspicion that she had been baiting him all along. He cupped her chin in his hand and turned her face to meet his, his eyes searching hers for any sign of hesitation. Finding none, he claimed her mouth in a fierce kiss, his tongue delving into the warm cavern of her mouth.

Jenna's hands reached up to tangle in his hair as she melted into him, her body responding to his touch like a wildflower to the sun. His free hand slid up her thigh, pushing her skirt higher and higher until he reached the damp fabric of her panties. He groaned against her mouth as he felt the heat emanating from her core. This was it; there was no turning back now. With one swift movement, he stood up and pulled her out of the chair, her body pressing against his, his erection straining against his trousers.

He pushed her back against the desk, his hands roaming over her body as he kissed her neck. Jenna gasped as his hands found her breasts, his thumbs flicking over her hardened nipples. He could feel her pebbled peaks through the thin material of her shirt, and he knew she wanted him just as badly as he wanted her. He broke the kiss and stepped back, his eyes raking over her body as he began to undo the buttons of her blouse. Jenna's breath hitched as she watched him, her eyes glazed with lust.

Her bra was next, and when it fell to the floor, her breasts spilled out, the perfect handful. Mr. Jameson took one in his mouth, teasing the sensitive bud with his tongue as Jenna arched her back, her hands gripping the edge of the desk for support. He could feel her body tremble against his, and he knew she was close to the edge already. But he didn't want it to end too quickly. He wanted to savor every moment, to explore every inch of her.

He kissed his way down her torso, his mouth leaving a trail of fire in its wake. He reached the waistband of her skirt and tugged it down, revealing the matching lacy thong she wore. Jenna stepped out of her skirt, now only in her thong and high heels, looking up at him with a mix of excitement and vulnerability. He hooked his thumbs under the elastic and pulled it down, her smooth skin bared to him. He stepped closer, his nose inhaling her sweet scent as he kissed the tops of her thighs.

Without wasting another second, Mr. Jameson knelt before her and pulled her closer to the edge of the desk. He took her panties in his teeth and pulled them aside, exposing her glistening pussy. He licked her slit from bottom to top, making her gasp and buck her hips. Jenna's legs began to shake as he found her clit and flicked it with the tip of his tongue. She grabbed his hair, pushing his face closer, silently begging for more. He eagerly obliged, his tongue delving into her warm, wet folds, tasting her sweetness as she moaned his name.

Her legs were trembling as she felt the first waves of an orgasm building. He stood up, his own need now overwhelming. He unbuckled his belt and pulled down his pants, freeing his rock-hard penis. Jenna's eyes widened as she took in the size of him, licking her lips in anticipation. He stepped closer, positioning the head of his cock at her entrance. "Are you ready for this, Jenna?" he growled, his voice thick with lust.

"Yes," she breathed, her voice shaky. "Please, Mr. Jameson." He pushed into her slowly, inch by inch, watching her face contort with pleasure and pain as he stretched her tight, young pussy. Once fully sheathed, he began to move, his hips pumping in a slow, steady rhythm. Jenna's nails dug into the desk as he filled her completely, the sound of their bodies slapping together echoing in the quiet room. She wrapped her legs around his waist, urging him deeper, her moans filling the air.

Mr. Jameson leaned over her, capturing her mouth in another scorching kiss as he picked up the pace. He could feel her tightening around him, her body preparing for release. He reached between them and began to rub her clit in time with his thrusts. Jenna's orgasm hit her like a tidal wave, her body convulsing around him as she cried out into his mouth. He didn't stop, instead, he pushed her through the waves of pleasure, her legs tightening around him as she climaxed over and over again.

Her body was still trembling from the force of her orgasms when he picked up the pace again, his strokes becoming more erratic and desperate. He could feel his own climax approaching, and he knew he wouldn't last much longer. "I'm going to cum," he grunted, his voice strained with pleasure. Jenna nodded, her eyes never leaving his. He pulled out again, this time moving to kneel beside the desk, his penis still hard and slick with their combined juices.

With one hand, he stroked himself, the other reaching for her stomach. He guided his cock to her belly button and began to pump his seed onto her, covering her in a warm, sticky mess.

The sight of his semen on her bare skin was too much for him, and he groaned as he continued to spurt, his hips jerking with every pulse of his release. Jenna's eyes went wide with shock and excitement as she felt the hot liquid spread over her stomach, pooling in her belly button.

Her own arousal spiked again at the sight, and she reached down to spread it over her skin, her fingertips sliding in the wetness. Mr. Jameson watched with a mix of satisfaction and hunger as she played with herself, her hand moving lower to stroke her clit. He knew she was close again, and he wasn't quite ready to be done with her yet. He leaned over and took one of her nipples in his mouth, sucking hard as she gasped.

With his other hand, he reached between her legs and slid two fingers into her, feeling the walls of her pussy contract around him. She was still sensitive from her previous orgasms, and she moaned loudly as he began to fuck her with his hand. Her eyes rolled back in her head, and she writhed on the desk, her body begging for more. He didn't disappoint, his thumb finding her clit and pressing down hard as he pumped into her. Her body tensed, and she came again, her pussy clenching around his fingers.

The feeling of her tightening around him pushed him over the edge, and he pulled his hand away to cover her in his cum. He watched as it spurted out in thick ropes, coating her stomach and breasts in a sticky, white blanket. Jenna looked up at him, her eyes glazed and her chest heaving with the force of her breaths. "Fuck," she whispered, the word filled with a mix of amazement and satisfaction.

Mr. Jameson collapsed beside her, his chest heaving as he tried to catch his breath. He looked down at the mess they had made, the evidence of their illicit tryst smeared across her skin and the desk. He couldn't help but feel a thrill of excitement knowing that no one would ever know what had happened here. It was their little secret, and the thought made him even harder.

But there was no time to rest. They had to clean up before anyone found them. He helped Jenna off the desk, his hands lingering on her still-bare ass. They quickly gathered their clothes and cleaned up the evidence of their passion, their movements efficient and silent. When they were both dressed, Mr. Jameson pulled Jenna into a tight embrace, his cock still semi-erect against her thigh.

He kissed her one last time before letting her go, his hand lingering on her shoulder. "I'll see you in class tomorrow, Jenna," he said, his voice a low murmur. She nodded, a small smile playing on her lips, and left his office, the echo of their passion still lingering in the air. Mr. Jameson sat down at his desk, his eyes on the now empty chair where Jenna had just been. He knew this was just the beginning of a very dangerous game they were playing, but he couldn't help but crave more of her sweet, young flesh.

Their secret trysts in his office became more frequent, their desire for each other growing stronger with every stolen kiss and furtive touch. They would have sex in class every now and then, the thrill of possibly being caught only adding to the intensity of their encounters. Jenna would come to his office after hours, her books and papers a flimsy pretense for the real reason she was there. They would fuck on the desk, the floor, even against the bookshelves, their moans muffled by the heavy door.

But Jenna was eager to learn more, to push her boundaries even further. She had always been curious about anal sex, and Mr. Jameson was more than willing to be her teacher. He knew that she would need time to get used to the idea, so he started slow, teasing her with just one finger as they lay together in the quiet of his living room after one of their private tutoring sessions. She was nervous at first, but his gentle touch and reassuring words soon had her relaxed and eager to explore this new realm of pleasure.

He began by massaging her inner thighs, his thumbs grazing her pussy before sliding up to her tight ass. He circled her anus with the tip of his finger, feeling her tense up. "Relax, baby," he cooed, his voice soothing and calm. "Trust me, I'll take care of you." He applied a bit of pressure, and she gasped as his finger slid inside her, the tight ring of muscle giving way to his gentle intrusion. Jenna's eyes went wide with surprise and a hint of pain, but she quickly found that she liked the sensation, the feeling of being filled in a way she never had before.

Mr. Jameson moved his finger in and out, adding another digit when she was ready. He took his time, watching her face for any signs of discomfort, his own desire for her building with every moan she made. When she was finally relaxed enough to take two fingers, he knew she was ready for the next step. He reached for the lube he had set aside earlier, squeezing a generous amount onto his thumb before returning to her tight little hole. He worked it in slowly, watching as she squirmed and gasped beneath him, her body adjusting to the new sensation.

He could feel her body start to open up, the muscles loosening around his digits. He whispered dirty things into her ear, telling her how much he wanted to fuck her ass, how much she was going to love it. Jenna's pussy was already wet, and he knew that she was close to orgasm again. He leaned down to kiss her, his tongue delving into her mouth as he pushed his thumb in deeper. She moaned into the kiss, her body arching towards him as she gave in to the feeling of fullness.

He could tell she was ready, and his own cock was painfully hard, begging for release. He pulled his fingers out and positioned himself behind her, the head of his penis nudging against her anus. He pushed in slowly, giving her time to adjust to the new sensation. Jenna's breath hitched, her body tensing as he entered her. But she didn't stop him, instead pushing back to take him deeper.

Mr. Jameson groaned with pleasure as her tight ass enveloped his cock, the feeling unlike anything he had ever experienced. He took it slow, inch by inch, until he was fully seated inside her. He paused, giving her a moment to get used to the sensation before he began to move. Jenna's moans grew louder, her body moving with his, eager for more.

He picked up the pace, his hips slapping against her firm cheeks as he fucked her ass. Jenna's hands were balled into fists in the couch cushions, her eyes screwed shut with the intensity of the sensations. He reached around to play with her clit, his fingers sliding through her wetness as he pushed into her. She was so tight, so hot, and he could feel his own orgasm building.

But he wasn't ready to let go just yet. He wanted her to come first, to feel the full force of anal pleasure. He leaned over her, his hand moving from her clit to her nipples, pinching and rolling them as he fucked her deeper. Jenna's moans grew louder, her body taut with the effort of holding back her climax. He knew she was close, and he wanted to be the one to push her over the edge.

With a final, gentle push, Mr. Jameson was fully inside her, his cock buried in her tight, virgin ass. He held still for a moment, giving her time to adjust, before he began to move again. Jenna's breathing was ragged, her body trembling with the effort to stay still. He leaned down to whisper in her ear, "You're so beautiful like this, baby. So perfect."

Her eyes snapped open, and she met his gaze in the mirror on the wall, her face a picture of pure ecstasy. He began to thrust into her in earnest, his hips moving in a steady rhythm that had her panting for breath. Her orgasm was building, the pressure in her ass intense and overwhelming. She reached down to touch her clit, her fingers slipping in her own juices as she stroked herself in time with his movements.

Mr. Jameson watched her in the mirror, his own pleasure mounting as he saw her losing control. He picked up the pace, his strokes becoming more urgent as he felt his own climax approaching. Jenna's eyes rolled back in her head, and she came with a scream, her body shaking with the force of her release. He followed soon after, his cock spasming as he emptied himself into her tight hole.

After a moment of panting and trembling, they separated, both of them glowing with the aftermath of their illicit encounter. Jenna looked up at him, a look of wonder in her eyes. "I never knew it could feel like that," she whispered. Mr. Jameson couldn't help but smile, feeling a sense of pride at being the one to show her this new experience.

Their relationship grew more intense over the next few weeks, their trysts becoming more frequent and daring. They had sex in class every now and then, the risk of being caught only adding to the excitement. But it was the private tutoring sessions at his home that Jenna truly craved. It was there that she could explore her deepest desires without the fear of judgment or discovery.

During one such session, Jenna decided it was time to take things even further. She had been thinking about it for days, the idea of Mr. Jameson's cock in her ass driving her wild with anticipation. She turned to him, her eyes filled with lust, and asked, "Could you teach me more?" He knew exactly what she meant, and his cock twitched at the thought of claiming her ass completely.

He led her to his bedroom, where he had set up a special area just for their sessions. He had pillows and blankets arranged to cushion her, and a bottle of lube within easy reach. Jenna lay down on her stomach, her legs spread, and Mr. Jameson began to massage her backside, his thumbs brushing against her anus teasingly. She gasped as he slid one finger inside her, feeling the familiar burn as she stretched around him.

He worked her slowly, adding another finger as she grew more comfortable. Jenna's breath grew ragged, her hips pushing back to meet his hand as he stretched her open. She knew what was coming next, and she was more than ready. She looked over her shoulder at him, her eyes pleading, "I want it all, Mr. Jameson."

He leaned down to kiss her, his cock aching with need. "You're going to get it, baby. I'm going to fuck your sweet little ass until you can't walk straight." Jenna's pussy clenched at his words, and she nodded eagerly, her body begging for the fullness she knew was to come. He applied more lube, coating his cock before he positioned himself behind her, the tip of his penis pressing against her now-ready hole.

With one firm push, he was inside her, the feeling of her tight ass around him more incredible than he could have ever imagined. Jenna's eyes watered with the pain, but she didn't tell him to stop. Instead, she pushed back, urging him deeper, her body already starting to adjust to the new sensation. Mr. Jameson began to move, his hips pumping into her with increasing speed and force.

The sound of their flesh slapping together filled the room, mingling with their moans and gasps. Mr. Jameson was in heaven, feeling Jenna's tight ass grip his cock like a glove. He had never felt anything so exquisite, so forbidden, and it was all the sweeter knowing that she was his student, that he was the one bringing her to these heights of pleasure. He reached down to play with her clit, his thumb circling the sensitive bud as he fucked her ass.

Jenna's moans grew louder, her body writhing beneath him as she approached another orgasm. He could feel her tightening around him, her muscles contracting with every stroke. "Yes, yes," she panted, her voice muffled by the pillow. "More, Mr. Jameson. Fuck me harder."

He didn't need any further encouragement. He grabbed her hips and began to pound into her, his cock sinking into the hilt with every thrust. She was so tight, so perfect, and he knew he wouldn't last much longer. He watched her in the mirror, her ass bouncing with every impact, and it was too much. With a roar, he came, his cum filling her up, the feeling of her tightness around him pushing him over the edge.

They collapsed onto the bed, their bodies tangled together in a mess of sweat and lust. Jenna's ass was sore, but in the best way possible. She couldn't believe how much she enjoyed it, how much she craved more of him inside her. She turned to look at him, her eyes still glazed with passion. "Thank you," she murmured, her voice soft and sultry. "Thank you for teaching me."

Mr. Jameson leaned in to kiss her, his hand cupping her cheek. "The pleasure was all mine, Jenna." He pulled out of her gently, watching as his cum leaked out of her ass. He couldn't help but feel a twinge of possessiveness, knowing that no one else would ever know the secrets she held. They lay there for a few moments, basking in the afterglow of their illicit encounter.

But reality was never far away. They had to clean up, return to their lives as teacher and student. They couldn't let anyone suspect what went on behind closed doors. With a sigh, Mr. Jameson helped Jenna to her feet, his eyes lingering on her naked body. He handed her a towel and watched as she wiped herself clean, her movements graceful and sensual.

They dressed in silence, the weight of what they had done hanging in the air. When they were both presentable again, Mr. Jameson opened the door to his office and peered out into the hallway. It was clear. They had gotten away with it again. He turned to Jenna, his voice low and filled with lust. "I'll see you in class tomorrow," he said, his eyes smoldering. "And maybe, if you're a good girl, we can do this again."

Jenna's heart raced at the thought of their next rendezvous. She nodded, her voice a whisper. "I'll be counting the minutes, Mr. Jameson." With that, she slipped out the door, leaving him with a view of her perfect ass as she walked away. He couldn't wait to claim it again, to feel her tightness around him once more.

Their secret continued, their desires growing more intense with every encounter. They had sex in class every now and then, the thrill of possibly being caught adding to the excitement. But it was the private tutoring sessions that truly set their hearts racing. At home, Mr. Jameson trained Jenna in the art of anal sex, starting with one finger and gradually working his way up to his cock. She was eager to please, her body responding to his every touch and command.

During one particularly heated session, Jenna decided to take control. She straddled him on the desk, her ass in the air, and began to lower herself onto his cock. Mr. Jameson's eyes went wide with shock and arousal as she took him inch by inch, her tight ass swallowing him whole. She moaned with every downward thrust, her cheeks red with excitement and exertion.

He watched in amazement as she rode him, her body moving in a way that was both innocent and incredibly seductive. He reached up to squeeze her breasts, his thumbs flicking her nipples as she bounced on his cock. The sight was too much for him, and he knew he wouldn't last much longer. "Fuck me, Jenna," he grunted, his hands gripping her hips as he thrust upwards to meet her.

Her movements grew faster, more erratic, and he could feel her tightening around him. He knew she was close. He leaned forward, his mouth finding her clit, and began to suck and lick as she fucked him. Jenna's moans grew louder, her body shaking as she reached for her own climax. "Yes, Mr. Jameson, yes!" she screamed as she came, her pussy contracting around his cock as she squirted all over his desk.

The sound of their moans filled the room, the scent of sex heavy in the air. He knew they had to be quiet, but it was difficult to keep his voice down when she felt so good. He pushed her off him, his cock still rock hard, and spun her around to face the desk. "I want you to bend over and take it like the good little slut you are," he growled, his voice filled with lust.

Jenna did as she was told, her hands gripping the edge of the desk as Mr. Jameson positioned himself behind her. He slid one hand down her spine to her ass, spreading her cheeks wide. He took a moment to admire her tight, pink hole before leaning in to kiss it gently. Jenna shivered with excitement, her body more than ready for what was to come.

He slid one lubricated finger into her ass, feeling her tense around him. He moved it in and out, getting her used to the sensation before adding a second. Jenna gasped, her pussy throbbing with every stroke. He could feel her getting wetter, her juices dripping down her thighs. He knew she was ready, so he pulled his fingers out and positioned his cock at her entrance.

With one swift thrust, he was inside her, the tightness of her ass gripping him like a vise. Jenna moaned into the desk, the pleasure mixed with a hint of pain. But she didn't stop him. Instead, she pushed back, taking him deeper, her body begging for more. Mr. Jameson began to move, his hips slapping against her ass as he fucked her hard.

Her moans grew louder, echoing through the room, and he knew he had to be careful not to get carried away. He reached around her, his hand finding her clit again, and began to rub it in time with his thrusts. Jenna's body responded immediately, her hips moving with him as she climbed towards another orgasm.

He watched in the mirror as she took his cock, her face a mask of ecstasy. He couldn't believe this was happening, that he was fucking his student's ass in his own home. But he didn't care. All that mattered was the feeling of her tight hole around him, the way her body trembled with every thrust.

Their secret encounters grew bolder, their passion uncontainable. They had sex in class every now and then, the thrill of possibly being caught making it all the more exhilarating. But it was at his home where Mr. Jameson truly began to train Jenna, pushing her boundaries and showing her the depths of pleasure she never knew existed.

One evening, after a particularly grueling session, Jenna lay on her stomach, her ass red and sore from his attentions. He had started with one finger, gently probing and stretching her until she was begging for more. He had added a second, then a third, until she was taking his entire hand. The feeling was unlike anything she had ever experienced, and she was insatiable for it.

He slid his fingers out of her and leaned over to kiss her, his breath hot on her neck. "You're doing so well, baby," he murmured, his voice filled with pride. "You're going to be the best little anal slut I've ever had." Jenna's pussy clenched at the thought, her body already craving his cock again.

He stood up, his erection pointing straight at her. "Get on your hands and knees," he instructed, his voice firm. Jenna complied, her heart racing with anticipation. He grabbed her hips and positioned himself behind her, the tip of his cock nudging against her well-used ass. She gasped as he pushed into her, the feeling of fullness overwhelming.

Mr. Jameson didn't waste any time, immediately starting to fuck her with deep, powerful strokes. Jenna's moans grew louder, filling the room as she lost herself in the sensation. She could feel her orgasm building again, her pussy throbbing with every thrust. He reached around her, his hand finding her clit, and began to rub it in a fast, circular motion.

Her body tensed, her muscles tightening around his cock as she came, her juices coating his shaft. Mr. Jameson groaned, his own climax approaching rapidly. He pulled out of her and flipped her onto her back, her legs spread wide. He took his cock in his hand and stroked it a few times, the head slick with her cum. Jenna watched with wide eyes as he brought it to her mouth, his other hand holding her head still.

"Suck me clean," he ordered, his voice strained. Jenna eagerly opened her mouth, taking his cock in as deep as she could. She licked and sucked, her tongue swirling around the head as he groaned in pleasure. She tasted herself on him, the musky scent of their combined release only making her more aroused. He watched her with a mix of lust and dominance, his hand tangled in her hair as he fucked her mouth.

Her eyes watered as he pushed deeper, but she didn't stop, her own hand moving to rub her clit as she took him all the way in. She felt his cock swell, knew he was close. With one final, deep throat, he pulled out and came all over her face and tits, his hot cum spurting out in thick ropes. Jenna closed her eyes, her body shaking with the intensity of it all.

They lay there for a moment, both panting and sweaty. Mr.

Jameson leaned down to kiss her, his tongue delving into her mouth to taste himself on her. She could feel his cock growing hard again, and she knew she wouldn't be able to resist. "Again?" she asked, her voice a needy whimper. He chuckled, his eyes dark with desire.

"Always, Jenna," he murmured against her lips. "Always." And with that, he rolled her over onto her stomach, his cock nudging at her still-sensitive ass. She moaned, already eager for more, as he began to push into her once again. The cycle of pleasure and pain continued, their secret meetings a never-ending dance of desire and submission.

The Aunty Next Door

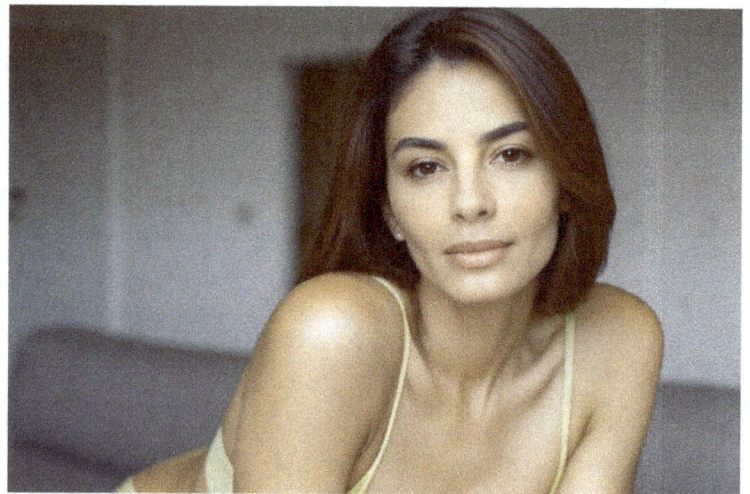

A warm, lazy afternoon washed over the quaint suburban neighborhood, and in one such unassuming house, Aunt Margaret lay sprawled out on her plush sofa, the soft fabric enveloping her ample curves. Her thoughts wandered to the sound of a basketball bouncing rhythmically outside her window, the only disruption to the quietude of her afternoon nap. She had noticed the new family that moved in next door a few weeks ago, but had yet to make their acquaintance. Her eyes fluttered open, and she peered out the window to see a young, shirtless boy practicing his layups. He was probably around 18, with a body that suggested a combination of teenage exuberance and burgeoning manhood.

Her gaze lingered on his taut abs and the way his shorts clung to his muscular thighs as he jumped and landed, each movement showcasing his athleticism. A faint blush crept up her cheeks as she allowed herself to indulge in the sight of his youthful vitality. Aunt Margaret had always had a soft spot for the boys in the neighborhood, but it had been years since she felt the stirrings of attraction that now began to unfurl in the pit of her stomach. She watched him, her heart rate quickening, as beads of sweat glistened on his tanned skin, the sun kissing his hairless chest with each bounce of the ball.

Her eyes traveled down to his crotch, where the outline of his growing arousal was becoming more pronounced with every move. It was clear that the young man was unaware of the effect he was having on her, lost in his own world of adolescent ambition. The sudden realization that she was openly ogling him sent a thrill down her spine, and she felt a slick wetness between her legs, her hand unconsciously moving to cup her own breast. She squeezed it gently, feeling the nipple harden under her palm as she imagined what it would be like to run her hands over his firm, young body.

Her thoughts grew increasingly daring, and she found herself contemplating the possibility of acting on her desires. After all, she was a mature woman with needs, and it had been a long time since she had felt the warmth of a man inside her. The idea of teaching him the ways of the world, of showing him the depths of pleasure that an experienced woman like herself could provide, was intoxicating. She sat up, smoothing her skirt over her plump thighs, and made a decision.

With a purposeful stride, Aunt Margaret walked to the front door, her mind racing with the tantalizing prospect of what was to come. She stepped outside and called out to the boy, her voice a seductive purr that belied her true intentions. "Young man, could you help me with something in the backyard?" she asked, her eyes gleaming with a mischief that had long been dormant. The boy looked over, his expression one of surprise and curiosity, and she couldn't help but smile at his innocence. Little did he know that his quiet afternoon was about to take a very adult turn.

He sauntered over, the basketball still bouncing at his side, his eyes never leaving hers. She led him through the gate and into the secluded space that she had cultivated over the years, a garden that was as lush and inviting as the desires she now felt. "I need someone strong and capable to help me move this heavy pot," she said, pointing to a large ceramic planter that was strategically placed beside a secluded bench, a knowing smile playing on her lips.

The boy set down his basketball and approached her, his eyes taking in her voluptuous figure with newfound interest. She could see the hunger in his gaze, and she knew that he was now aware of the sexual tension that crackled in the air between them. "Let me help you," he offered, his voice a low rumble that sent a shiver down her spine. They both grasped the pot, their fingers brushing against each other's, and she took the opportunity to press her body against his, feeling the heat of his skin through his thin shorts.

With a feigned grunt, she allowed her hand to slip down to his waist, her palm resting on the firmness of his ass. His breath hitched, and she could feel his cock stirring as she whispered in his ear, "Why don't you sit down and take a break?" She gestured to the bench, and he complied, his eyes never leaving hers as he sat down. She straddled him, her skirt hiked up to reveal her plump, bare thighs, and she took his face in her hands, bringing his lips to hers in a fiery kiss that spoke of years of pent-up passion.

His hands roamed up her body, cupping her breasts and squeezing them gently, his thumbs flicking at her sensitive nipples. She moaned into his mouth, feeling the ache in her core grow stronger with every touch. As they kissed, she reached down and pulled at the waistband of his shorts, freeing his hardened penis. It sprang forth, eager and unyielding, and she took it in her hand, stroking it with a slow, practiced rhythm that made him gasp. "You like that, don't you?" she murmured, her voice thick with desire, and he nodded, his eyes glazed with lust. "Good," she said, her teeth grazing his earlobe, "because I'm about to show you what it feels like to be with a real woman." She knelt before him, her eyes never leaving his as she took his length into her mouth, her tongue swirling around the head before she took him deeper, her cheeks hollowing as she sucked. He bucked his hips, a moan escaping his lips, and she knew she had him right where she wanted him. This was just the beginning of a steamy, educational affair that would leave them both breathless and begging for more.

Her mouth worked magic on his cock, her experience shining through as she teased and tormented him with her tongue and teeth. She could feel him growing harder, his breathing becoming ragged, and she knew it was time to take things to the next level. She stood, her legs trembling slightly with anticipation, and turned to face the bench, her ample ass sticking out towards him. "Take me from behind," she instructed, her voice husky with need. "But first, I want you to taste me." She bent over, her skirt riding up to expose her wet, glistening pussy, and he needed no further prompting. He leaned forward, his tongue darting out to trace the length of her slit before he buried his face between her legs, his tongue delving deep inside her. She moaned loudly, her hips moving back and forth as he ate her out with a hunger that matched her own.

When she could bear it no longer, she pushed him away and turned to face him, her chest heaving. "Now," she demanded, her voice a growl, "I want you inside me." He didn't hesitate, standing and positioning himself behind her. He took a moment to appreciate the view, his cock poised at her entrance, before he pushed forward, filling her up in one smooth, powerful stroke. She gasped at the sensation, her body stretching to accommodate his girth, and she pushed back against him, urging him deeper. He began to thrust, the sound of their flesh slapping together filling the quiet afternoon air. She could feel her orgasm building, each movement sending waves of pleasure crashing through her body.

As they fucked, Aunt Margaret reached between her legs, her fingers finding his tight, puckered ass. She slipped one inside, preparing him for what was to come. His moans grew louder, his hips moving faster as she explored his virgin hole. She knew that once she had him fully at her mercy, she would show him the true meaning of pleasure. "Do you like that?" she asked, her voice taunting, and he could only nod, his breath coming in pants. She added another finger, scissoring them apart to make way for her ultimate goal. "Good," she whispered, "because I'm about to show you a whole new world, baby." And with that, she pulled his cock from her pussy and guided it to her tight, untouched anus, pushing back until he was fully seated in her ass, her muscles clenching around him in a vice-like grip.

The boy's eyes went wide, his hands gripping her hips tightly as she began to rock back and forth, taking him deeper into her body. He had never experienced anything so intense, so taboo, and it was driving him wild. His cock felt like it was on fire, the sensation of her ass muscles rippling around him unlike anything he had ever felt before. Aunt Margaret leaned back, her breasts bouncing as she worked herself onto his cock, her own pleasure mounting with every thrust. She reached around to stroke his balls, her other hand playing with her clit, the combination sending her closer and closer to the edge.

They moved together, their bodies in perfect harmony, their cries of pleasure echoing through the garden. She felt his cock swell inside her, and she knew he was close. "Come for me," she panted, her voice hoarse with passion. "Come deep inside my ass." And with that, he lost control, his hips bucking as he filled her with his hot, thick cum. She screamed out her own climax, her pussy clenching around his balls, her body shaking with the force of it. They collapsed onto the bench, panting and sweaty, their hearts racing in tandem.

For a moment, they stayed like that, their bodies still joined, the only sound their ragged breaths and the distant chirp of birds. Then Aunt Margaret pulled away, her hand still resting on his ass, her eyes gleaming with satisfaction. "You see," she said, her voice soft and sultry, "you're not just a boy anymore. You're a man who knows what he wants." She licked her lips, her eyes never leaving his. "And I know what you want. You want me to keep teaching you." He nodded, his voice barely a whisper. "Good," she said, standing up and straightening her skirt, "because I've only just begun." She turned and walked back towards the house, leaving him on the bench, his cock still hard and his mind racing with the promise of what lay ahead.

The next few weeks were a whirlwind of erotic education for the young man. Aunt Margaret taught him everything she knew, from the art of oral sex to the delights of anal play, pushing his boundaries and showing him the depths of his own desires. They fucked in every corner of the house, in every position imaginable, their clandestine affair becoming the highlight of both their days. And as the summer sun grew stronger, so did their passion, burning hot and unstoppable, leaving them both gasping for more. But little did he know that his Aunt had many more lessons in store for him, and she was eager to share her vast knowledge of the carnally pleasurable world that awaited.

One day, as he was helping her in the kitchen, she leaned over the counter, her ample breasts spilling out of her blouse, and whispered something into his ear that made him blush furiously. "Tonight," she said, her eyes sparkling with mischief, "I want you to fuck me in front of a mirror." The thought of watching their bodies joined, seeing every inch of her that he had only felt before, was almost too much for him to handle. He nodded eagerly, his cock already hardening at the prospect.

That evening, they retreated to her bedroom, the curtains drawn tight to keep their secret hidden from prying eyes. She led him to a full-length mirror and had him lie on the bed, her own body straddling his as she lowered herself onto his cock. The sight of their reflection was almost as arousing as the act itself, her plump breasts bouncing in time with his thrusts, their faces contorted in pleasure as they watched each other's every move. It was a visual feast that only served to heighten their arousal, each of them eager to explore new ways to drive the other wild.

As their bodies moved in unison, Aunt Margaret reached for a bottle of lubricant she had placed on the nightstand earlier. She coated her hand before sliding it between their bodies, her fingers finding his tight asshole. He gasped as she pushed one inside, the sensation foreign and thrilling all at once. She began to pump her hand in time with her movements on his cock, her eyes never leaving his in the mirror as she introduced him to the pleasure of prostate stimulation. His eyes rolled back in his head, and he could feel himself getting closer and closer to the edge, his body tightening in anticipation of the orgasm that was building deep within him.

The moment he came, she pulled her hand away, her own climax following shortly after, her pussy clenching around his still-hard cock. They lay there, panting and slick with sweat, staring at their reflection in the mirror. The look of awe and satisfaction on his face was all the confirmation she needed that she had indeed made him a man. But their journey was far from over, and she had so much more to show him. With a wink and a kiss, she whispered, "Tomorrow, I'll introduce you to toys," and the excitement in his eyes told her that she had a very eager pupil.

The following afternoon, with the curtains drawn once more, Aunt Margaret pulled out a velvet-lined box from her dresser, revealing an assortment of sex toys that made the young man's eyes go wide with wonder. She picked out a sleek vibrator and a butt plug, explaining their uses with a wicked smile. "Tonight, we're going to learn about the joy of simultaneous pleasure," she said, her voice a siren's call that had him eagerly agreeing to whatever she had in store.

They started with the vibrator, her showing him how to tease her clit with it, her body quivering as she demonstrated. Then she handed it to him, guiding his hand as he took over, watching in the mirror as he brought her to a screaming orgasm. The sight of his cock, red and pulsing with need, was almost too much for her to bear, and she begged him to enter her again. This time, she inserted the butt plug, the feeling of fullness making her gasp and her pussy even wetter.

As they fucked, the vibrations from the plug resonated through her body, making each thrust feel like heaven. He watched in the mirror as his cock disappeared into her, her ass cheeks clenching around him, and he knew he had never felt anything so incredible. The sight of the toy sticking out of her, the way it made her moan and squirm, was almost too much to handle. He pounded into her, his own orgasm approaching like a freight train, and when it hit, he could feel her pussy contract around him, milking him for every last drop.

They collapsed onto the bed, their bodies entangled and hearts racing. The room was filled with the scent of their sex, and the quiet hum of the vibrator on the floor was the only sound that broke the silence. As they lay there, their breathing slowly returning to normal, Aunt Margaret whispered, "You see, there's so much more to discover, so much more to enjoy." He nodded, his eyes glazed with lust and adoration. He was hers, completely and utterly, and she intended to make sure he knew every inch of her body, every sensation she could give him.

Their secret trysts continued, each one more intense than the last. They tried new positions, new toys, and even ventured into the realm of bondage, her guiding hand and sultry voice leading him down the path of ecstasy. And with each passing day, their connection grew stronger, their need for each other more insatiable. They had stumbled upon something rare and beautiful, a connection that transcended their age gap and societal norms, and they were both all too willing to indulge in its forbidden fruits.

One evening, as the light danced across their naked bodies, she whispered, "Tonight, I want you to watch me," her voice a velvet promise that had him instantly hard. She slid off the bed and onto the floor, her legs spread wide, and began to masturbate, her eyes locked on his in the mirror. He watched, mesmerized, as she touched herself, her fingers moving with a confidence that was both erotic and empowering. She brought herself to the brink, her body trembling, before turning to him with a knowing smile. "Now, it's your turn," she said, and he eagerly took his place, her eyes on him as he stroked his cock, watching his every move.

Their gazes met in the mirror, and she leaned back against the bed, her legs still spread wide, inviting him to join her. He approached, his cock glistening with precum, and she took his hand, placing it between her thighs. Together, they brought themselves to a crescendo of pleasure, their eyes never leaving their reflection as they came together in a symphony of passion and desire.

In those stolen moments, Aunt Margaret taught the boy next door the true meaning of sexual liberation, and he became her devoted student, eager to learn every lesson she had to offer. And as the summer days grew shorter, the fire between them burned brighter, their secret garden of lust a sanctuary from the mundane world outside.

Professor OLIVIA

EROTICA SHORT STORIES

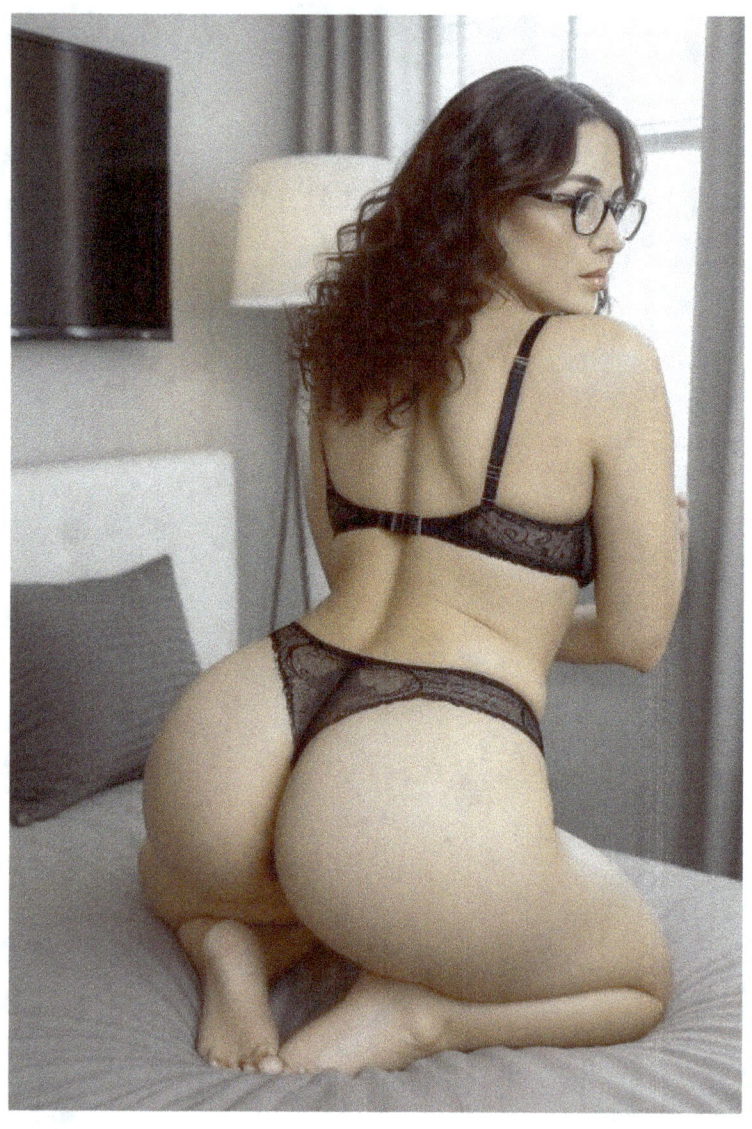

PROFESSOR OLIVIA

The first day of the new semester at the prestigious Westwood University had arrived, and the air was buzzing with the excitement of young minds eager to absorb knowledge. Among the throngs of students shuffling through the hallways was Liam, a 21-year-old junior with a penchant for literature and an insatiable appetite for life's carnally sweet experiences. Little did he know that his dull, mundane world was about to be rocked by the sudden appearance of a new substitute professor, Olivia. She was a vision of beauty and intelligence, standing tall at 5'7" with a figure that could make the most stoic of scholars swoon. Her long, auburn hair cascaded down her back, framing her porcelain skin and piercing blue eyes. Her full, round boobs strained against the fabric of her tight-fitting blouse, and her ass, oh her ass, was a masterpiece of nature that could make the most chaste of men commit sins of the flesh.

Olivia, at 29, was a recent graduate of the same university with a PhD in English Literature. She had an air of authority and confidence that was only magnified by the way she carried herself, walking with the poise of a gazelle and the allure of a siren. She stepped into the classroom, her heels clicking rhythmically on the tiles, and the students' whispers died down as they took in her presence. She introduced herself as Professor Hart, her voice a smooth blend of honey and gravel that seemed to resonate deep within Liam's soul. He found himself inexplicably drawn to her, his eyes lingering on her shapely legs as they peeked out from under her pencil skirt.

The flirtation between them grew with every passing lecture, their glances lingering a touch too long, their smiles a tad too knowing. It was during one particularly steamy afternoon, as the sun streamed through the windows and the heat of the room seemed to thicken the very air, that the tension finally snapped. After class, as the last student shuffled out, Liam lingered, pretending to organize his notes. He watched as Olivia bent over her desk, her skirt riding up to reveal the tops of her stockings and the sweet curve of her ass. It was all he could do to keep his hands to himself. But when she turned and caught him staring, her expression shifted from one of irritation to something else entirely.

"Mr. Daniels," she said, her voice a low purr, "I think we have some… extra curricular matters to discuss."

Liam's heart raced as he watched Olivia saunter towards him, her hips swaying with a hypnotic grace that had his mouth watering. He felt a sudden, overwhelming need to taste her, to touch her, to claim her in a way that was far beyond the confines of the classroom. The way she looked at him, with those piercing blue eyes that seemed to see straight through to his very soul, sent a shiver of desire down his spine.

"Follow me," she murmured, her voice a siren's song that he had no power to resist. She led him through the deserted hallways, her hand brushing against his as they made their way to the staff restroom. The moment they were safely ensconced in the last stall, the air crackled with the electricity of their shared want. He reached for her, his hands shaking slightly as he cupped her breasts, feeling their weight and softness through the fabric of her blouse.

Olivia's breath hitched as Liam's thumbs grazed her nipples, already hard and eager. She leaned into his touch, her body arching towards him like a plant reaching for the sun. She felt his arousal pressing against her, thick and insistent, as his hands slid down to her waist, his fingers tracing the line of her skirt. He tugged at the material, pulling it up to expose her lacy underwear, and she stepped out of it, letting him admire her nakedness. She felt a thrill of power, knowing she had this young, virile man in the palm of her hand.

Olivia reached down and began to undo his pants, her hand sliding into his boxers to grasp his hardening penis. He gasped as she began to stroke him, her touch firm and confident, a clear indication that she was no stranger to the art of seduction. She dropped to her knees, her eyes never leaving his as she took him into her mouth, her tongue swirling around the tip before she took him deeper, her cheeks hollowing as she sucked him with a hunger that left him trembling. He felt the urge to thrust into her mouth, but she maintained control, her hand gripping the base of his shaft as she worked him over with her lips and tongue.

As she stopped to breathe, his own hands found their way under her skirt, his fingers slipping between her legs to feel the heat and wetness of her pussy. She was already soaking wet for him, and the realization sent a bolt of pure lust coursing through his body. He stroked her gently, teasing her clit with the pad of his thumb, feeling her hips buck against his hand as she grew more and more aroused. He could feel her pulse racing through the soft, velvety folds of her sex, and he knew she was close to climax. He slid a finger inside her, her walls tightening around him as she moaned into his crotch.

The sound of her pleasure was like music to his ears, and he found himself on the edge as well. But Olivia had other plans. She stood up abruptly, her cheeks flushed and her eyes gleaming with desire, and pushed him onto the closed toilet lid. With deft movements, she straddled him, her skirt hiked up to expose her matching lace panties. She leaned in and whispered into his ear, "I've wanted this since the moment I saw you, Liam." Then, with a seductive smile, she pulled her panties aside and lowered herself onto his throbbing penis, her vagina enveloping him in a warm, wet embrace that made him grit his teeth with pleasure.

He watched as her boobs bounced with every movement she made, the sight of them driving him wild. He reached up to cup them, his thumbs flicking at her erect nipples, drawing gasps from her as she began to move faster and faster. The feeling of her tight, slick heat was indescribable, her muscles rippling around his shaft as she rode him. He could feel her juices coating him, the evidence of her need for him making his own desire burn even brighter.

Liam's hands slid down her back, his fingertips digging into her flesh as she ground herself against him, her movements becoming more erratic as she chased her release. He felt his own orgasm building, the pressure in his balls reaching a fever pitch. He looked up at her, his eyes glazed with lust, and whispered, "I'm going to come, Professor."

Olivia's smile grew wicked as she leaned in closer, her breath hot on his skin. "Not yet, Liam," she murmured, her voice a silken promise. "We have all afternoon." And with that, she reached between them and began to stroke his balls, the gentle pressure sending shockwaves of pleasure through his body. She knew just what she was doing, her experience and knowledge of the human form allowing her to manipulate his responses with a mastery that left him panting.

As she rode him, Olivia reached behind and slid a finger into her own anus, the sensation making her moan with pleasure. Liam's eyes widened in surprise, but the sight of her exploring her own body only served to increase his arousal. He watched, entranced, as she worked herself, her cheeks flushing a deep shade of pink that matched the color of her brazen lust. The sound of their bodies slapping together echoed in the small space, mingling with the occasional gasp or moan that slipped from their lips.

Feeling the need to take control, Liam stood up, lifting Olivia with him. She wrapped her legs around his waist, her ankles locking at the small of his back as he pinned her against the stall door. The change in angle was exquisite, the friction of their bodies driving them both to new heights of pleasure. He began to thrust into her, hard and fast, the sound of his hips smacking against her ass echoing through the room. She met each of his movements with eager enthusiasm, her nails digging into his shoulders as she matched his rhythm.

Olivia's moans grew louder, her breath coming in short, panting gasps as she felt her climax building. She tightened her legs around him, urging him deeper, her pussy clenching around his cock as she neared the edge. Liam's own need was reaching a crescendo, his strokes growing more erratic as he felt the pressure in his balls tighten. He knew he wouldn't last much longer, but he was determined to bring her to the brink first.

With a final, powerful thrust, he reached between them and pinched her clit, the sudden sensation sending her spiraling over the edge. She screamed his name, her body convulsing in pleasure as waves of ecstasy washed over her. The feel of her orgasm triggered his own, and he erupted deep inside her, filling her with his hot, pulsing seed. They held each other, their bodies trembling in the aftermath of their shared climax, their breathing ragged and their hearts racing.

For a moment, they remained like that, locked in their passionate embrace, the rest of the world forgotten. But reality soon began to seep back in, the sound of distant footsteps and the knowledge that they could be caught at any moment sending a thrill of illicit excitement through them both. They quickly straightened their clothes, Olivia smoothing down her skirt with a secret smile playing on her lips.

"Meet me at my place tonight," she murmured, her voice a seductive whisper that sent a shiver down his spine. "We have much more to discuss… and explore."

Liam could only nod, the words 'Yes, Professor' dying on his lips. The thought of spending the evening in her embrace, exploring every inch of her body, was almost too much to handle. He stumbled out of the bathroom, his thoughts a whirlwind of lust and anticipation. The rest of the day was a blur of half-hearted attempts at concentration, his mind wandering back to the steamy encounter in the stall at every opportunity.

When the sun began to set, casting the campus in a warm, golden glow, Liam found himself standing outside Olivia's apartment, his nerves a jumbled mess. He took a deep breath and knocked on the door, his heart pounding like a drum in his chest. The door swung open to reveal her standing there, a vision in a simple black dress that clung to her curves like a lover's caress. Her hair was down, cascading over her shoulders in soft waves, and she had applied a touch of makeup that only served to enhance her natural beauty.

"Come in," she purred, her eyes raking over his body in a way that made him feel both vulnerable and incredibly desired. The apartment was dimly lit, candles flickering on the coffee table and the faint scent of jasmine in the air. She led him into the living room, where a bottle of wine and two glasses sat waiting.

They talked for a while, the conversation flowing easily between them as they sipped their wine. But the tension between them was palpable, a live wire just waiting to be touched. They circled each other, their eyes speaking a language that needed no words, until Olivia set her glass down and took his hand.

"Let's move this to the bedroom," she murmured, pulling him towards the hallway. He followed willingly, his heart racing in anticipation. The room was bathed in soft light, the bed a sea of plush pillows and silky sheets. She turned to face him, her dress slipping to the floor to reveal a matching set of lingerie that left little to the imagination.

Olivia stepped closer, her breasts brushing against his chest, and kissed him deeply. Her tongue danced with his, a passionate dance that seemed to have been rehearsed for an eternity. He felt himself growing hard again, his body responding to her touch as if it had been programmed to do so. They tumbled onto the bed, a tangle of limbs and passion, their kisses growing more frantic as they touched and explored each other.

Her hands found his zipper, deftly releasing his cock from the confines of his pants. It sprang free, already thick and eager, and she took it in her hand, her grip firm as she began to stroke him. He moaned into her mouth, his hips bucking up to meet her touch. She broke the kiss, her eyes locking onto his as she began to lower her head, her tongue tracing a wet path down his chest, over his stomach, and finally to his throbbing erection.

Her mouth was heaven, pure and simple, and he could feel himself losing control as she took him in, her lips sliding over his length with a practiced ease that spoke of countless hours of pleasure-giving. He watched, transfixed, as she pleasured him, her eyes never leaving his as she worked her magic. He reached down to cup her breasts, his thumbs brushing over her hardened nipples, and she let out a low moan that sent a shiver of pleasure through his body.

Olivia's hand found his balls, her gentle touch sending waves of sensation through him. He knew he wouldn't last much longer, but he wanted to savor every second of this moment, to burn it into his memory so he could relive it over and over again. He felt the pressure building, his orgasm approaching like a freight train, and he tightened his grip on her hair, urging her to go faster, to push him over the edge.

And then she did, taking him deep into her mouth and sucking hard as she stroked his shaft. The sensation was too much, and he came with a roar, his body arching off the bed as he spilled into her mouth. She swallowed greedily, her eyes never leaving his as she milked the last drops of his pleasure.

When he had finished, she licked her lips and climbed up to straddle him, her own need clear in the way she rocked her hips against his sensitive flesh. "My turn," she whispered, a mischievous smile playing on her lips as she reached for the nightstand drawer. She pulled out a condom and a bottle of lubricant, her gaze never leaving his face as she ripped the foil packet open with her teeth and slid the latex over his still-hard cock.

With a slow, deliberate movement, Olivia squeezed a generous amount of lube onto her fingers, coating them in the slick substance before sliding them down to her own sex. Liam's eyes followed her every move, his chest heaving with the effort to control his ragged breathing. She slid a digit into her vagina, her eyes fluttering shut as she moaned softly, and then another into her tight, unexplored ass. She was preparing herself for him, and the sight was almost too much for him to bear.

He watched as she began to work her fingers in and out, the sounds of her wetness mixing with her quiet gasps of pleasure. The sight of her touching herself, her body reacting so visibly to his presence, was more erotic than anything he had ever experienced. His cock jerked against his stomach, begging for release, and he reached out to touch her, to be a part of the intimate moment.

Olivia took his hand and brought it to her mouth, sucking his fingers clean before guiding them to her clit. "Show me how much you want me," she whispered, her voice a siren's call that he couldn't resist. He began to stroke her, his touch tentative at first, but growing bolder as she responded to him, her hips rising to meet his hand. Her breathing grew ragged, her moans filling the room as she approached the peak of her pleasure.

And then she was there, her body tightening around her own hand as she came, her juices coating her thighs. She slid her fingers out of her pussy, offering them to him, and he tasted her, the flavor of her desire making him grow even harder. He wanted more, needed more, and he knew that she felt the same.

Without a word, she turned around and presented her ass to him, her pussy glistening with arousal. She bent over the side of the bed, one hand braced against the mattress, the other reaching back to spread her cheeks. "Take me," she breathed, the words a command and a plea all rolled into one.

PROFESSOR OLIVIA

Liam didn't need any more encouragement. He slid the condom onto his cock and positioned himself behind her, his hands on her hips as he guided himself to her entrance. He pushed in slowly, feeling the tightness of her ass clench around him as he filled her completely. She was so warm, so tight, and the sensation was unlike anything he had ever felt. He began to move, his hips slapping against her firm cheeks as he claimed her in the most primal of ways.

Olivia's moans grew louder, her body moving back to meet his thrusts with an eagerness that was intoxicating. He could feel her muscles contracting around him, her orgasm building again. He reached around and found her clit, his thumb stroking it in time with his movements, the dual sensation driving her wild.

Their rhythm grew more frantic, the sound of skin on skin and the slick sound of their joining filling the room. They were lost in their own little world of lust and desire, two souls joined in the most intimate of dances.

As Olivia's second climax neared, her walls tightened around him, squeezing him in a vice-like grip that threatened to shatter his control. He felt his own orgasm building, the pressure in his balls growing with each thrust. He knew he wouldn't be able to hold out much longer, the intensity of the sensation threatening to overwhelm him.

And then it hit, a wave of pleasure so intense it was almost painful. He roared as he came, his hips bucking as he emptied himself into her, the force of his release making her body convulse around him. They held onto each other, their bodies trembling in the aftermath, their breaths coming in gasps.

For a moment, they remained like that, connected in the most intimate of ways. Then Olivia pulled away, her eyes shining with satisfaction as she turned to face him. "Now," she said, a wicked smile playing on her lips, "we can truly begin our lessons."

Next Door Boys

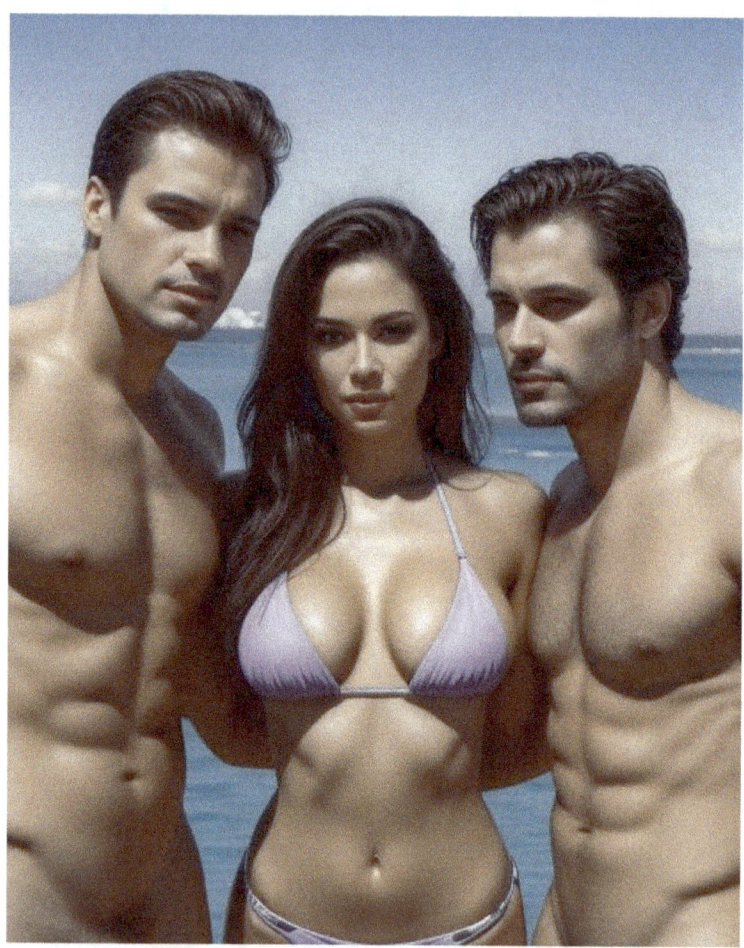

Lila, a sweet, innocent-looking 18-year-old with a fiery spirit that often went unnoticed by the townsfolk. Her long, raven hair cascaded down her back in soft waves, and her emerald eyes sparkled with mischief when she knew she was about to get what she wanted. And what she wanted tonight was her boyfriend next door, Jake, who had just turned

19.

Jake, with his chiseled abs and a cocky smile that could melt the most stubborn of hearts, had been Lila's neighbor and secret crush for as long as she could remember. With his blond hair and piercing blue eyes, he had the kind of charm that could make any girl drop her panties at the mere suggestion of it.

The two of them had been flirting for months, their attraction palpable whenever they passed each other on the street or at school. Finally, on this sultry summer evening, they had found themselves alone in Jake's bedroom, the tension between them thick enough to cut with a knife. Lila had come over under the guise of borrowing a book, but it was clear that neither of them had reading on their minds.

Jake's twin brother, Ethan, who shared the same room, had gone out with friends, leaving the lovers with the perfect opportunity to explore their desires. The air was heavy with lust as Lila leaned in, her full, pink lips brushing against Jake's ear, whispering sweet nothings that sent shivers down his spine. His hand found its way to her waist, pulling her closer, and she could feel his hardened member pressing against her.

The moment their eyes met, the dam of desire broke, and they were lost in a passionate kiss that seemed to swallow the world around them. Jake's hands roamed her body, cupping her breasts through her shirt and teasing her erect nipples. Lila moaned into his mouth, her hands fumbling with the button of his jeans, desperate to feel his skin against hers.

Their clothes fell away in a tangled mess, leaving them naked and exposed. Jake's penis stood tall and proud, a testament to his excitement. Lila took it in her hand, stroking it gently as she looked up at him with a mix of awe and hunger. She had never seen anything so beautiful and powerful.

Jake's breath hitched as she took him into her mouth, her tongue swirling around the tip, tasting his arousal. He groaned, his hand entwined in her hair as he guided her movements. Meanwhile, his own hand traveled down to her vagina, exploring her slick folds, finding her clit and giving it a gentle squeeze.

Their passion grew with each touch, each kiss, each caress. Lila felt herself getting wetter by the second, her body begging to be filled by him. Jake could feel her heat and knew she was ready. He laid her back on the bed, his body hovering over hers as he positioned himself at her entrance. He looked into her eyes, questioning, and she nodded eagerly, biting her bottom lip in anticipation.

With one swift thrust, he entered her, and Lila gasped at the sensation of being stretched to accommodate his size. She had been with a couple of guys before, but none had ever made her feel this way. Jake's eyes never left hers as he began to move, his hips rocking back and forth in a steady rhythm that had her legs trembling. Her nails dug into his back as she arched off the bed, meeting each of his thrusts with her own.

The sound of their flesh slapping together filled the room, mingling with their moans and gasps of pleasure. Lila's vagina clenched around him as he hit that perfect spot inside her, sending waves of pleasure crashing through her body. Jake's own moans grew louder as he felt her tighten around him, his own orgasm building.

But fate had other plans for this steamy encounter. The door to the bedroom swung open, revealing Ethan, who had returned earlier than expected. Caught in the act, Lila and Jake froze, their eyes wide with shock and embarrassment. Ethan, however, did not look away. His gaze was fixated on the sight before him, his own arousal evident in his eyes.

For a moment, the room was silent, save for the heavy breathing of the trio. Then, Ethan's expression morphed from surprise to something darker, something hungrier. He stepped into the room, closing the door behind him with a gentle click that echoed through the tension-filled air.

"Looks like you two don't need that book after all," Ethan said, his voice low and filled with amusement. Lila blushed a deep crimson, trying to cover herself with the discarded blanket, while Jake remained frozen, his penis still buried deep inside her.

Ethan took a step closer, his eyes roving over their entwined bodies with a mix of curiosity and desire. "I don't think I've ever seen a more beautiful sight," he murmured, and Lila felt a strange thrill at his words.

"Ethan, I'm so sorry," she stammered, trying to pull away from Jake, but he held her in place, his arms like steel around her waist. "It's not what it looks like," Jake said, though his voice was strained, his hips still moving slightly with the rhythm of their passion.

Ethan chuckled, the sound sending a shiver down Lila's spine. "I think it's pretty clear what's happening here," he said, taking another step closer. "But I'm not mad, if that's what you're worried about." He paused, his eyes traveling down to where they were joined. "In fact, I'd say you're both about to get a little more than you bargained for tonight."

Lila's heart raced as she processed the situation. She had never considered the possibility of a threesome before, but the idea of having both brothers, her long-time crush and his twin, inside her was too tempting to resist. She looked into Jake's eyes, seeking reassurance, and found it in the lustful fire that burned there. He gave her a small nod, and she relaxed back into the pillows, her legs spreading wider.

Ethan approached the bed, his eyes never leaving their joined bodies. He reached out and gently traced a finger along Lila's cheek, his touch sending a jolt of electricity through her. He leaned in and kissed her, his tongue sliding past her lips, tasting the hint of Jake's essence. Lila's eyes fluttered closed, overwhelmed by the sensation of being kissed by two men at once.

Jake's rhythm increased, his hips slamming into her as he watched his brother kiss her. The sight was intoxicating, and he found himself growing harder than ever before. He knew Ethan had always had a wild streak, but he never imagined this would be the night it came out to play.

Ethan's hand traveled down her body, his fingers finding their way to Lila's clit. He began to rub her in slow circles, matching the pace of Jake's thrusts. Lila moaned into Ethan's mouth, her body responding instinctively to the dual pleasure. It was as if they had rehearsed this moment a thousand times, their movements in perfect sync despite the spontaneity of it all.

Without breaking the kiss, Ethan reached over and took one of Lila's breasts in his hand, rolling the nipple between his thumb and forefinger. She arched her back, pressing into his touch, and Jake took the opportunity to kiss and suck on the neglected peak. Her body was a symphony of sensation, each touch and kiss adding to the crescendo building within her.

Ethan's hand continued to work magic between her legs, and she felt her orgasm approaching like a runaway train. She tightened around Jake, her walls pulsing with need. He groaned into her neck, feeling her clench around him, and that was all it took for him to lose control.

He thrust into her one final time, his warm seed filling her up as he climaxed. But Ethan wasn't done yet. He pulled away from her mouth and moved down her body, his tongue tracing a wet path from her neck to her navel, then lower. He positioned himself between her legs, his eyes meeting hers as he licked along the length of Jake's shaft, still buried inside her.

Lila's eyes went wide with surprise and desire as she watched Ethan pleasure her. Jake slowly withdrew, giving his brother full access to her dripping wet pussy. Ethan didn't waste a second, plunging his tongue into her depths, tasting the mixture of their juices. Lila's legs quivered, and she let out a keening cry as Ethan began to feast on her, his tongue dancing and flicking over her sensitive clit.

The room was filled with the sound of wet, sloppy kisses and Lila's desperate moans. She had never felt so alive, so wanted, so utterly consumed by pleasure. As Ethan brought her closer and closer to the edge, she reached down and took Jake's cock in her hand, stroking him back to hardness, eager for more.

The twins looked at each other over her body, a silent understanding passing between them. This was just the beginning of a night that would change all of their lives forever, a night that would be etched in their memories as the hottest summer evening of passion and discovery.

Ethan's tongue swirled around Lila's clit as Jake's hand took over the rhythmic stroking of her inner thigh. They moved in unison, each touch and lick designed to drive her wild. Lila's body tensed, and she could feel the orgasm building, threatening to shatter her into a million pieces.

And then it hit her, a wave of pleasure so intense it was almost painful. She screamed out, her body convulsing as Ethan lapped at her, drinking in her release. Jake watched in amazement, his own arousal growing with each spasm that wracked her body.

As Lila's orgasm subsided, Ethan slid up the bed, kissing his way back to her mouth. They shared the taste of her, and she could feel the heat of their passion growing once more. She reached for Jake, her hand caressing his still-hard cock, and whispered, "I want both of you."

The twins shared a knowing smile, their eyes sparkling with mischief. Jake rolled onto his back, his cock standing tall and proud. Ethan positioned Lila on top of him, her legs straddling his waist, and then he moved behind her, his own erection pressing against her ass.

Lila took a deep breath, her heart racing with excitement. She had never been with two guys at once, but she trusted the twins implicitly. As she lowered herself onto Jake, Ethan's lubricated tip brushed against her anus, sending a shiver up her spine. She felt a moment of trepidation, but the desire to explore her boundaries was too strong to resist.

With gentle coaxing from Ethan, she relaxed and allowed him to push into her, inch by inch. The sensation was unlike anything she had ever felt before—both exquisitely pleasurable and slightly painful. But the way Jake's eyes bore into hers, filled with love and lust, made her feel safe and cherished.

The twins began to move in sync, their cocks sliding in and out of her in a rhythm that was as natural as breathing. Lila's moans grew louder, her hips rocking back and forth to meet theirs. The feeling of fullness was overwhelming, her vagina and ass stretched to accommodate them both.

Jake's hands gripped her hips, guiding her movements as Ethan's hands caressed her back, occasionally reaching around to tweak her nipples. The room was a whirlwind of sensations, and Lila felt herself spiraling closer to another climax. She could feel their hearts beating in unison, the three of them connected in a way she never thought possible.

Their bodies moved together, a dance of passion and need. Lila's breath hitched as Ethan's penis hit a spot inside her that no one had ever found before, sending sparks of pleasure shooting through her. Jake took advantage of her distraction, sliding his thumb down to her clit, sending her hurtling over the edge once more.

Her walls tightened around them, and the twins could feel her orgasm wash over them like a tidal wave. They picked up their pace, their hips moving in perfect harmony as they chased their own releases. The sweat glistened on their bodies, a testament to their exertion.

Ethan was the first to go over the edge, his body tensing as he roared out his climax, filling her ass with his hot seed. Lila could feel the pulsing of his cock, sending aftershocks of pleasure through her body. Jake wasn't far behind, his orgasm hitting him like a freight train.

With a final, powerful thrust, he filled her vagina with his cum, the two brothers marking her as their own. They stayed connected, their breathing heavy and ragged, the aftermath of their shared pleasure leaving them all momentarily speechless.

As they lay there, tangled in a web of limbs and satisfaction, Lila couldn't help but feel a sense of completeness she had never experienced before. It was as if she had found a piece of herself in the arms of these two incredible men.

The night grew late, and the candles flickered, casting shadows over their spent bodies. They lay together, the air still thick with lust and love. It was clear that this was just the start of a new chapter in their lives, one filled with passion and exploration.

And as they drifted off to sleep, their bodies entwined in a tapestry of desire, Lila knew that she would never look at summer evenings—or the boys next door—the same way again.

Mysterious Couple Next Door

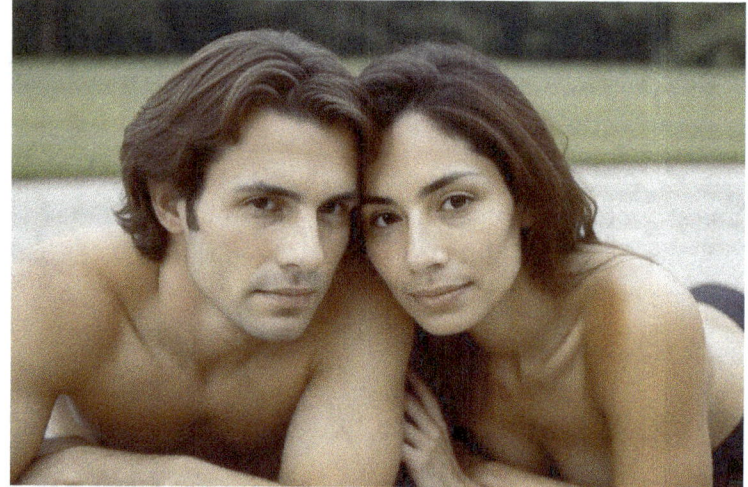

Emma, the young and curious girl next door, had always been fascinated by the allure of the mysterious couple that had moved in a few months ago. They were both attractive in their mid-thirties, and their passion for one another was palpable, even from the confines of her own home. She had caught glimpses of them in their backyard, their laughter and whispers carrying through the open windows during the warm summer evenings. Tonight, however, was different. The couple, Mark and Rachel, had set the stage for something far more intimate.

It had started innocently enough. The moon was high and full, casting a soft, silver glow over the lush, green grass. The air was thick with the scent of blooming flowers and the distant hum of nightlife. Emma, unable to resist the allure of the quiet night, found herself peering through the crack in her curtains, her eyes drawn to the couple lounging on the large, red outdoor sofa. Rachel's long, brunette hair cascaded over Mark's broad chest as he traced his fingers along the inside of her thigh. Rachel's eyes fluttered closed, her mouth parted slightly as she leaned into his touch.

Emma felt a peculiar heat in her cheeks and a tingling in her lower belly as she watched Mark's hand slip under Rachel's skirt, revealing a hint of lacy lingerie. Rachel's hand reached up to gently cup the back of Mark's head, pulling him closer. His mouth found hers in a deep, hungry kiss. Emma's own breath hitched as she watched their bodies press together, the fabric of their clothes the only barrier between their heated skin. Rachel's hand slid down to Mark's crotch, her fingers squeezing and caressing the growing bulge.

As the intensity of their embrace grew, Mark's hand moved to Rachel's chest, cupping her firm breasts in his palms. Rachel moaned into the kiss, arching her back and pushing herself into his touch. Emma's own breasts swelled and her nipples hardened, her hand unconsciously moving to mirror Rachel's. Rachel's dress slipped down, revealing her erect nipples and Mark's mouth descended to greet them. Rachel's legs parted slightly, giving Emma a glimpse of her shaved pussy, glistening with arousal in the moonlight.

The sight was almost too much to handle. Emma's hand moved down, her fingers finding the slick wetness between her own legs. She was surprised at how eagerly her body responded to the show playing out before her. Rachel's hand was now working at the button of Mark's pants, his hard penis springing free. Emma had never seen one in person before, and the sight of it made her heart race. Mark's hand guided Rachel's to his shaft, and she began to stroke him with an expert touch that left no doubt as to their shared intimacy.

As Rachel took Mark's penis into her mouth, Emma felt a sudden jolt of arousal, her own hand moving faster. Rachel's eyes closed in pleasure, her cheeks hollowing as she took him deeper. Mark's hand found Rachel's pussy, his fingers teasing her clit before plunging into her wet warmth. Rachel's moans grew louder, and Emma realized that she was no longer watching a private moment; she was a participant in their erotic dance, her own body responding to their every move.

But what she didn't know was that Mark and Rachel had noticed her watching. They had seen her shadowy form in the window from the beginning, and their performance was for her benefit. The couple had been waiting for the perfect moment to introduce their young neighbor to the delights of adult play, and it seemed that night had arrived.

Mark's eyes flicked up to meet hers, holding her gaze even as Rachel's mouth worked his length. He gave her a knowing smile, his eyes sparkling with mischief. Rachel looked up, her eyes locking onto Emma's, and she moaned around his cock as she winked. It was a silent invitation, one that sent a thrill of excitement through the young girl. Rachel's hand slid down to her own pussy, her fingers moving in a slow, tantalizing rhythm.

Emma's eyes went wide with shock and arousal, but she couldn't look away. Rachel was putting on a show, her body moving sinuously with every stroke of Mark's hand and every suck of her mouth. The couple's openness and the raw passion on display was intoxicating. Rachel's other hand reached behind her, unhooking her bra and letting her breasts fall free. They bounced slightly as she bobbed her head, the nipples dark and hard with desire.

Mark stood up, his erect penis pointing straight at Emma. Rachel looked up at him, licking her lips, and whispered something in his ear. He nodded and turned to face the window, Rachel following his lead. Rachel spread her legs wider, exposing her pussy completely. Mark knelt between them, his tongue darting out to taste her. Rachel's hand reached out, beckoning Emma to join them. The unspoken invitation was clear: they wanted her to be part of this.

The decision was made in a split second. Emma's hand stilled on her clit, her breathing shallow. She knew she should turn away, but she found she couldn't. Rachel's eyes never left hers as Mark began to lick her pussy with an enthusiasm that had Rachel's body writhing on the sofa. Rachel's hand reached for her own breasts, playing with her nipples as Mark's tongue delved deeper. The sounds of their lovemaking filled the night, and Emma felt her own desire growing, demanding release.

With trembling legs, she stepped out of her bedroom and into the darkness of her backyard. The couple on the sofa didn't stop, didn't even look up. They knew she was there, and they continued their erotic performance, their bodies moving in perfect harmony. Rachel's hand reached down to guide Mark's penis into her pussy, her eyes never leaving Emma's. The sight of them joined together was more than Emma could bear. She stumbled forward, her hand reaching out to touch Rachel's thigh. Rachel's hand found hers, pulling her closer.

The moment their skin touched, it was as if an electric current passed between them. Rachel's hand guided Emma's to Mark's cock, still slick with her juices. Rachel whispered, "Stroke him," and Emma obeyed, her hand tentative at first but growing bolder as Rachel's hand showed her the rhythm. Mark groaned into Rachel's pussy, the vibrations sending waves of pleasure through her. Rachel's hand reached out to cup one of Emma's breasts, her thumb flicking over the hard nipple.

Their threesome was a dance of seduction, each touch and caress calculated to bring the young girl into their fold. Rachel's moans grew louder as Mark's thrusts grew more urgent, and Emma felt her own body responding, her pussy aching to be filled. Rachel leaned back, her eyes locked on Emma's as she reached down to touch her own clit, her movements frantic.

Mark pulled out of Rachel, his cock glistening with her wetness, and turned to face Emma. Rachel whispered, "Take his cock," and Emma, driven by a desire she didn't understand, straddled Mark, feeling the head of his penis against her own slick entrance. Rachel's hand guided her down, and Emma gasped as she felt him fill her completely, stretching her in a way she had never been before. The pleasure was intense, and she began to ride him, her hips moving in time with Rachel's hand on her clit.

The night grew hazy with passion, their bodies moving together as if they had been lovers for years. Rachel's mouth found Emma's breast, her teeth grazing the sensitive flesh as Mark's cock pounded into her. The sensation was overwhelming, and Emma's eyes rolled back in her head as Rachel's tongue flicked over her nipple. Rachel's hand guided Emma's hips, urging her to match Mark's rhythm, and Emma felt a warmth spread through her that she had never experienced before. Rachel's eyes never left hers, the older woman's gaze filled with a fiery desire that only seemed to fan the flames of Emma's own passion.

Suddenly, Rachel pulled away, standing up and leading Emma by the hand to a nearby chair. She bent the younger girl over, her hands on her hips, and whispered, "It's time for you to experience the fullness of us." Mark took his place behind Rachel, his cock now pressing against Emma's ass as Rachel reached down to spread her cheeks. Rachel leaned in, her breath hot on Emma's ear, "Are you ready?" The question was more of a command, and Emma nodded, her body quivering with anticipation. Rachel's hand slid down to stroke Emma's clit, making her gasp as she felt Mark's penis at her entrance, the tip of it teasing her anus. Rachel whispered, "Relax, sweet girl," and pushed a finger into her, preparing her for the new sensation.

Emma tensed, but Rachel's soothing voice and the exquisite pleasure of her stroking her clit had her melting into the chair. With Rachel's help, Mark pushed the head of his cock into Emma's ass, the feeling of being filled there both strange and exhilarating. Rachel's fingers danced around her pussy, and Emma felt herself opening up, allowing Mark to slide in deeper. Rachel's hand slipped away from her clit and reached back to guide Mark's movements, ensuring that every inch was met with the perfect amount of pressure and pleasure.

Their bodies moved in unison, the sound of skin slapping against skin echoing through the night. Rachel leaned over, her breasts pressing into Emma's back as she kissed her neck. "You're doing so well," she murmured, her breath hot and heavy. "We're going to make you feel so good." Rachel's hand found Emma's clit once again, her fingers moving in circles that had Emma's orgasm building. Mark's thrusts grew harder and faster, and Rachel's hand matched the tempo, pushing her closer and closer to the edge.

Emma's moans grew louder, and she felt Rachel's hand slide away from her clit, only to be replaced by something bigger and harder. Rachel whispered, "You're going to come for us, aren't you?" and Emma nodded, unable to form words. Rachel's fingers entered her pussy, filling her completely, and Emma felt herself come apart, her body shaking with the most intense orgasm she had ever experienced. Rachel's hand continued to pump in and out of her, her thumb pressing down on her clit, drawing out every last drop of pleasure.

And then it was Rachel's turn. She climbed onto the chair, straddling Mark's face, her pussy hovering just above his mouth. Mark eagerly licked and sucked, Rachel's juices mixing with his saliva as he devoured her. Rachel's cries grew more frantic, and Emma watched in amazement as Rachel's body convulsed in pleasure. Rachel's orgasm washed over her, her pussy clenching around Mark's tongue. Rachel's hand reached down to stroke Emma's clit once more, and Emma felt herself coming again, her pussy clenching around Rachel's fingers as she rode the wave of ecstasy.

As Rachel climbed off Mark, she looked at Emma with a knowing smile. "You're one of us now," she said, her voice thick with lust. And Emma, still trembling from her orgasm, knew that she had crossed a threshold she could never return from. The girl next door had become the couple's plaything, and she had never felt more alive. The night was still young, and the promise of more pleasure lay ahead, the three of them entwined in a web of desire that had no intention of letting any of them go.

Rachel took Emma's hand, leading her back to the sofa. Mark followed, his cock still standing at attention, his eyes never leaving the young girl's body. Rachel lay down, her legs spread wide, inviting Emma to take her place between them. Emma felt a thrill of power as she straddled Rachel's face, her own pussy now wet with the juices of her first anal experience. Rachel's tongue darted out, licking up her own cum mixed with Mark's precum, and Emma felt an instant jolt of pleasure.

Their eyes met as Rachel's tongue explored her folds, and Emma realized she was in control. She began to move her hips, riding Rachel's face, her moans growing louder with every flick and suck. Rachel's hands reached up to cup her ass, pushing her down harder onto her mouth, urging her to go faster. And as Rachel's tongue danced across her clit, Emma felt Mark's hands on her hips, guiding her down onto his waiting cock.

He filled her once again, this time with ease, and she moaned into Rachel's mouth, the feeling of fullness overwhelming. Rachel's hands moved to her own breasts, squeezing and playing with her nipples as she licked and sucked at Emma's clit. The sensation was indescribable, and Emma knew she was going to come again. Rachel's tongue delved deeper, pushing into her pussy as Mark's cock filled her ass, and she felt a pressure building, a coil of pleasure that had no end.

Her body tightened, muscles clenching, and then she was falling, screaming with pleasure as Rachel's mouth worked her clit and Mark's cock slammed into her. Rachel's hands gripped her ass, her tongue lapping at her pussy, and Mark's hands found her breasts, his fingers rolling her nipples. The world around her shattered into a million pieces of light as she came, her body spasming with the intensity of it. Rachel's muffled moans vibrated against her pussy, and Emma felt Mark's cock pulse inside her, his own climax following quickly.

The three of them lay tangled together, panting and spent. Rachel's eyes gleamed with satisfaction, Mark's chest heaving with exertion. Emma felt a sense of belonging she had never experienced before. She had been seduced by the couple next door, and she had never been more willing to surrender to them. As they held her, their bodies still joined, she knew that this was just the beginning of a long, passionate journey.

They slept for hours, when Emma woke up she felt Rachel's hand on her inner thigh, gently caressing her. The moon had set, and the room was filled with the soft glow of early dawn. Rachel's eyes were open, watching her, and Emma felt a warmth spread through her body that had nothing to do with the sun rising outside. Rachel leaned in and kissed her softly, her tongue slipping into her mouth, tasting her.

Emma's hand found Rachel's breast, her fingers playing with the soft flesh, feeling the nipple harden against her palm. Rachel's hand slid down to Emma's pussy, her fingers finding her clit, and Emma moaned into the kiss. Rachel broke away, her eyes twinkling with mischief. "Where's Mark?" she whispered, her voice thick with sleep and lust.

Emma looked around, feeling a sudden shyness wash over her. Rachel chuckled, a sound that sent shivers down her spine. "Don't worry, sweetie, he'll be out soon." And with that, Rachel began to kiss her way down Emma's body, her tongue tracing a wet line from her neck to her navel. Mark chose that moment to emerge from the bathroom, a towel wrapped around his waist, his body still glistening from the shower.

He smirked as he saw Rachel with her face buried between Emma's thighs, and Emma's cheeks flushed with arousal as he dropped the towel, revealing his fully erect penis. Rachel looked up, her eyes meeting Mark's, and she gave his cock a playful lick before returning to her task. Mark's smirk grew as he watched Rachel's tongue delve into Emma, the younger girl's moans growing more desperate with every stroke.

Emma's body was a canvas of sensation, Rachel's tongue painting exquisite patterns across her swollen clit, Mark's fingers exploring her still-tight ass. She felt so open, so exposed, and yet she had never felt more alive. Rachel's hands moved up to her breasts, her thumbs circling the hard peaks as she licked and sucked, her mouth never leaving Emma's pussy.

"I think she's ready for another round," Rachel murmured, her voice muffled by the flesh she was worshipping. Mark's eyes gleamed with excitement, his cock bobbing in anticipation. Rachel sat up, her own breasts bouncing slightly with the movement. She took Mark's hand and guided it to Emma's ass, whispering, "Prepare her."

Emma felt a thrill of fear and excitement as Mark's lubricated fingers began to probe her anus. Rachel's mouth returned to her pussy, her tongue flicking and teasing as Mark's fingers worked her ass open. The sensation was strange, but Rachel's attentions kept her arousal at fever pitch. Rachel's eyes never left hers, her gaze intense and filled with a hunger that matched Mark's.

Mark's thumb pushed past the tight ring of muscle, and Emma gasped as Rachel's tongue delved into her pussy. Rachel's hand found her own clit, her movements growing more erratic as she watched Mark claim Emma's ass. "You're going to take both of us now," Rachel murmured, her voice hoarse with passion.

"Are you ready, baby?"

Emma nodded, her eyes wide with excitement. Rachel's hand moved to Emma's clit, her thumb circling the sensitive bud as Mark's cock began to push into her ass. The feeling was indescribable, the pressure and the stretch almost too much to bear. But Rachel's tongue and Mark's gentle coaxing had her body relaxing, accepting him.

Their movements grew more synchronized, Rachel's thumb moving in time with Mark's thrusts, their eyes locked together as they brought her closer and closer to the edge. Rachel's other hand slipped into her own pussy, her fingers matching Mark's rhythm as he pushed deeper into Emma's ass.

The pressure grew, and Emma felt her body tense, her muscles clenching around Mark's cock. Rachel's thumb moved faster, pressing down harder, and then she felt it, the wave of pleasure crashing over her. Rachel's mouth moved to her clit, sucking and nibbling as Mark's cock filled her completely.

The room was filled with the sounds of their passion, their bodies moving together in perfect harmony. Rachel's moans grew louder, and Emma felt her own orgasm building, a pressure that threatened to consume her. Rachel's hand gripped her hip, her mouth moving to Emma's clit as Mark's hand found Rachel's pussy.

The three of them were lost in their own world, a dance of desire that had no end in sight. Rachel's orgasm washed over her, her body convulsing around Mark's cock, her mouth still working Emma's clit. And then, with a final, desperate thrust, Mark filled her with his cum, his hands tightening on her hips.

The room was silent, their heavy breathing the only sound as they lay tangled together, Rachel's mouth still on Emma's pussy, Mark's cock buried in her ass. Rachel looked up, a wicked smile on her lips, and whispered, "Again?"

Emma's eyes fluttered open, meeting Rachel's, and she nodded, her voice a breathy whisper. "Yes," she said, "I'm ready for another round." Rachel's smile grew, and she began to kiss her way back up her body, her tongue leaving a trail of fire in her wake.

The day had barely begun, but for Emma, it had already been a night of unparalleled passion. She knew that this was only the beginning of a journey that would take her to heights she had never dreamed of. Rachel's hand found her clit again, and Emma arched her back, ready for whatever came next.

Rachel sat up, her breasts swaying with the movement, and took Mark's cock into her hand. She stroked him slowly, her eyes never leaving Emma's. "It's your turn, sweetheart," Rachel purred, and Emma felt her pussy clench with excitement. Rachel's hand guided her down to Mark's cock, the head of it still slick with their combined juices.

Emma took him in her mouth, her eyes still locked with Rachel's. Rachel's hand moved to her own pussy, her fingers slipping in and out, setting a rhythm that Emma eagerly matched with her mouth on Mark's cock. Rachel's moans grew louder, and Emma felt a sense of pride that she could bring this woman, this goddess of lust, such pleasure. Mark's hands found her breasts, his thumbs rolling her nipples as Rachel watched, her breath hitching with every stroke.

Rachel leaned back, her hand moving from her pussy to her clit as Emma continued to suck Mark's cock. Rachel's eyes never left hers, and Emma felt a connection forming between them, a bond that went beyond mere physical attraction. Rachel's orgasm built, her hips bucking as her hand moved faster and faster. And just as Rachel's body convulsed with pleasure, Emma felt Mark's cock swell in her mouth, and she took him deep, swallowing every drop of his cum as he came with a roar.

They lay there, the three of them, panting and satisfied, their bodies intertwined. Rachel reached down to stroke Emma's cheek, her eyes filled with a warmth that went beyond the lust of the moment. "Welcome to our world," Rachel whispered, and Emma knew she had found her place.

The days turned into weeks, and the threesome grew more adventurous with every encounter. They explored every inch of one another, pushing boundaries and discovering new heights of pleasure. Rachel taught Emma the art of seduction, showing her how to use her body to bring a man to his knees. Mark taught her the power of submission, showing her the joy in letting go and letting someone else take control.

Emma found herself craving the feel of Rachel's mouth on her pussy, the way Rachel's tongue could coax an orgasm from her with ease. And Mark's cock, the way it filled her so completely, was a constant source of wonder. She had never felt more alive, more desired, more loved.

Their secret affair grew bolder with every passing day, their passion for each other spilling out into their every interaction. The neighbors began to whisper, but they didn't care. They were in their own little bubble, a world of pleasure that no one could touch.

One evening, as they lay together, Rachel looked at Emma with a glint in her eye. "There's one more thing we need to teach you, baby," she said, her hand sliding down to Emma's ass. "You've taken us both in every way but one."

Emma's heart raced as Rachel's fingers circled her tight hole. Rachel leaned in and whispered, "It's time for your final lesson in pleasure." And with that, Rachel's lubricated fingers pushed into her ass, stretching her open as Mark's cock slid into her pussy once again. The feeling was intense, but Emma's body had become accustomed to their games, and she welcomed the sensation.

Rachel's tongue traced a line up her spine as Mark's cock filled her completely, and Emma felt a new level of ecstasy building inside her. Rachel's hand reached around, her thumb pressing against her clit, and Emma's body began to spasm. Rachel's voice was a gentle command in her ear, "Come for us, baby," and Emma did, her orgasm ripping through her like a storm.

Their love grew stronger with every shared moment, every whispered secret, every shared climax. They were three bodies, moving as one, their hearts beating in unison. And as they lay there, their sweat mingling in the warm night air, Emma knew that she had found her true home, in the arms of the couple next door.

Friends sister

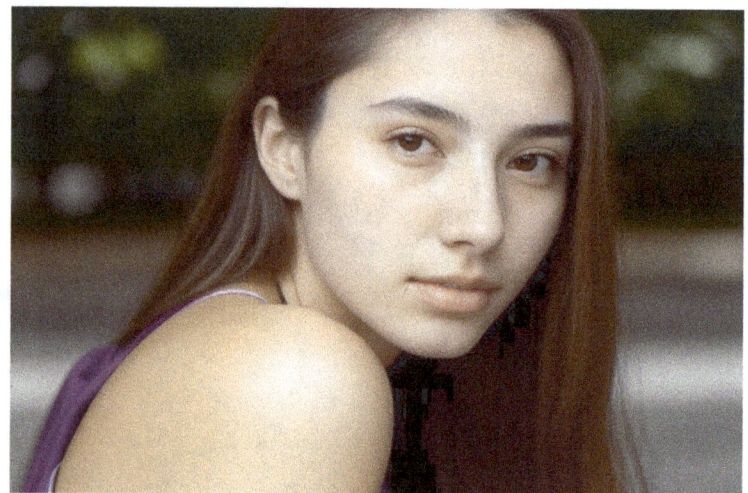

The air was thick with the sweet scent of blooming flowers as Mark strolled down the cobblestone path leading to his best friend's house. The sun cast a warm glow on the quaint cottage, its ivy-covered walls hinting at secrets that had been whispered through the generations. Inside, Mark's friend, Tom, was away on a week-long business trip, leaving behind his younger sister, Emily, to watch over the place. Emily was a beauty, with fiery red hair that cascaded down her back, a figure that could make any man's heart race, and emerald eyes that sparkled like the most precious of jewels.

As Mark approached the front door, his thoughts drifted to the many times he had fantasized about her. The way she moved with such grace, the gentle curve of her hips, and the way her breasts bounced with every step she took. His pulse quickened at the thought of the unexplored territory that was Emily's body, and the prospect of being alone with her sent a shiver of excitement down his spine. He had always been drawn to her, but had never dared to act on his desires, fearing the repercussions of crossing that sacred bond of friendship.

Upon entering the house, he was greeted by the faint sound of music coming from the backyard. Following the melody, he found Emily lying on a lounge chair, her eyes closed, basking in the warmth of the afternoon sun. Her skin glistened with a light sheen of sweat, and she wore nothing but a skimpy bikini that barely contained her ample assets. The sight of her made Mark's cock swell with desire, straining against the fabric of his shorts. He took a deep breath, trying to compose himself, and called out a casual greeting.

Emily's eyes snapped open, and she sat up, a smile playing on her lips as she recognized the voice. "Mark!" she exclaimed, her cheeks flushing a delicate shade of pink. She quickly adjusted her bikini top, the fabric slipping slightly to reveal the swell of her left breast. He couldn't help but stare, his eyes drawn to the tantalizing glimpse of flesh.

"I didn't expect you," she said, her voice a little breathless. "Tom mentioned you might come by, but I didn't think it would be so soon."

Mark took a step closer, his eyes never leaving hers. "Yeah, I had some free time on my hands and thought I'd come say hello," he replied, his voice thick with desire. He could see the curiosity in her gaze as it flickered down to the bulge in his shorts and back up to meet his eyes again.

Emily's smile grew more knowing, and she stood up, the movement causing her breasts to jiggle slightly. "Would you like a drink?" she offered, swaying her hips as she walked to the patio table where a pitcher of lemonade sat. The way her bikini bottoms hugged her curves made Mark's mouth water. He nodded, his eyes following her every move.

As she poured the drinks, Mark stepped closer, his eyes tracing the lines of her body. He could see the outline of her nipples, hard from the cool breeze, and the way her bikini barely covered her pussy. The anticipation was killing him, and he knew he had to act soon or risk losing his nerve. "You know," he said, his voice low and seductive, "I've always had a bit of a…crush on you, Em."

Emily's hand paused mid-pour, the ice clinking in the glass as she turned to face him. "Is that so?" she asked, a playful lilt to her voice. "And what exactly does that entail?"

Mark took the drink from her hand, setting it down on the table with a gentle thud. "Well," he began, stepping closer to her until there was barely an inch of space between them. "It involves a lot of late nights, thinking about what it would be like to touch you." He reached out and brushed a strand of hair from her face, his fingertips grazing her cheek.

Emily's eyes searched his, a hint of surprise and excitement in their depths. She licked her lips, her breathing becoming more shallow. "And what would it be like?" she asked, her voice barely above a whisper.

"It would be like this," Mark murmured, leaning in to capture her mouth with his own. His tongue slid against hers, exploring the sweetness of her lips as his hands found the ties of her bikini top. With a gentle tug, the fabric loosened, and her breasts spilled out, the nipples standing erect and begging for his touch. He cupped them in his hands, feeling their weight, rolling the nipples between his thumbs and forefingers, watching her eyes darken with lust.

Emily's hands found his waist, her nails digging into his skin as she moaned into his kiss. She could feel the heat from his cock pressing against her stomach, and she knew that she wanted him as badly as he wanted her. Her hand snaked down to grip him through his shorts, the warmth and size of him making her knees weak. "Take me inside," she breathed, pulling him toward the house.

Once inside, they stumbled through the living room, leaving a trail of discarded clothing in their wake. Mark's hands roamed over her body, exploring every inch of her smooth, sun-kissed skin. They reached her bedroom, the door slamming shut behind them. He laid her down on the bed, his eyes feasting on her naked form. He kissed his way down her neck, her breasts, and her stomach, his tongue tracing the path to the apex of her thighs. He could feel the dampness of her pussy, and his cock ached to be inside her.

Without a moment's hesitation, Mark positioned himself between her legs. He took his cock in hand and guided it to her wet entrance. Emily's eyes never left his as he pushed into her, filling her completely. She gasped, her body stretching to accommodate his size, and wrapped her legs around his waist. He began to move, his hips pumping in a steady rhythm that made her moan with pleasure. The sound of their bodies slapping together filled the room, punctuated by her gasps and his grunts of effort.

The sensation was overwhelming, and Emily could feel an orgasm building deep within her. Her pussy clenched around his shaft, and she bucked her hips up to meet him, urging him deeper. Mark's eyes were dark with lust as he watched her face contort in pleasure. He knew he was close as well, his balls tightening with each stroke. He reached between them, finding her clit with his thumb, and began to rub it in circles as he continued to fuck her.

Emily's moans grew louder, and she arched her back, her breasts thrusting upward as she climaxed. Her body trembled beneath him, her pussy pulsing around his cock, and Mark couldn't hold on any longer. He thrust into her one last time, burying himself to the hilt, and came with a roar. His hot seed filled her, the sensation sending waves of pleasure through her body. They lay there for a moment, both of them panting and trying to catch their breath, their bodies slick with sweat and desire.

Their eyes locked, and Mark knew that he had crossed a line that could never be uncrossed. But in that moment, all he cared about was the feeling of her tight, wet warmth surrounding him, and the knowledge that he had finally claimed the woman he had desired for so long. He leaned down to kiss her again, his cock still buried inside her, and she responded eagerly, her legs still wrapped around his waist.

He began to move again, slower this time, savoring the connection between them. Emily's hips rolled in time with his, her pussy still quivering from the aftershocks of her orgasm. Mark felt himself growing hard again, and he knew he wasn't done with her yet. He pulled out of her and flipped her over onto her stomach, spreading her legs wide apart. He kissed his way down her spine, his teeth grazing her skin, making her shiver.

Reaching around, he cupped her breasts from behind, kneading them gently as he lined his cock back up with her entrance. With one hand, he reached down and spread her ass cheeks, revealing her tight little asshole. He spit into his hand and lubricated her anus, watching her tense up in anticipation. "You're so beautiful," he murmured, his voice thick with desire. "I've always wanted to take you here."

Emily looked over her shoulder at him, her eyes wide with a mix of fear and excitement. "Do it," she breathed, her voice shaky. "I want you to."

Mark didn't need any further encouragement. He slid the tip of his cock into her ass, feeling the tightness grip him like a vice. She let out a sharp gasp, but he didn't stop, pushing in inch by inch until he was fully seated. She was so tight that he could feel every muscle in her body tense and relax around him as she adjusted to his girth. He began to move again, his strokes long and slow, letting her get used to the sensation of being filled in a way she never had before.

Emily's moans grew louder as she pushed back against him, taking him deeper with each thrust. He reached around to stroke her clit again, the dual sensation of his cock in her ass and his fingers on her clit driving her wild. Her orgasm built again, this time more intense than the first, and she screamed his name as she came, her body shaking with pleasure.

Mark felt her tighten around him, and he couldn't hold back any longer. He pulled out and turned her onto her back, his cock glistening with her juices. He stroked himself a few times before aiming at her face, and with a final groan, he shot his load, covering her in a warm, sticky spray. Emily licked her lips, tasting him, and the sight of her doing so pushed him over the edge again, and he came even harder, his cock pulsing with every spurt.

They lay there, tangled in the sheets, their bodies still trembling with the aftermath of passion. Mark knew that this was only the beginning of a journey that would change their lives forever, but for now, all that mattered was the feeling of her in his arms, the taste of her on his lips, and the memory of their bodies joined as one. He leaned down to kiss her again, and she melted into him, her eyes closed in pure bliss. They had crossed the line, and there was no going back.

Free Use Girl

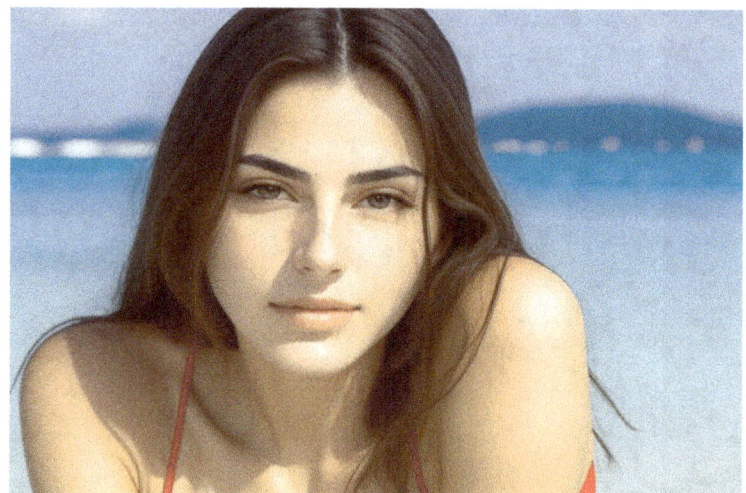

John had heard the whispers for months. His curiosity piqued, he found himself drawn to the enigmatic aura that surrounded the girl next door, Rachel. Her reputation as a "free use" girl was the talk of the neighborhood, a siren's call to his ever-present adolescent desires. Rachel, a young woman in her early twenties, had a certain charm that seemed to invite the most intimate of encounters with the men who sought her out. Her house, a small, unassuming abode, had become the epicenter of illicit whispers and secret rendezvous.

The warm summer evening beckoned him with a tantalizing promise of fulfillment. The air was thick with anticipation, and the crickets chirped in rhythm with the throbbing of John's pulse. He had made up his mind, tonight would be the night he would act upon his urges. Rachel's house loomed before him, a beacon of taboo pleasure, and his steps grew heavier with each passing moment.

John's palms were slick with nerves as he knocked on Rachel's door. It swung open almost immediately, revealing Rachel dressed in nothing but a thin, almost transparent negligée that barely concealed the ample curves of her breasts and the swell of her hips. She looked at him with a knowing smile, her eyes sparkling with mischief.

"Come in, John," Rachel purred, stepping aside to let him enter.

The interior of Rachel's house was dimly lit, the air suffused with the sweet scent of vanilla and jasmine candles. The walls were adorned with erotic art, and the faint sound of a jazz record played in the background, setting a sultry mood. Rachel closed the door behind him and took his hand, leading him to the plush velvet sofa that sat in the center of the living room.

John's heart raced as Rachel sat down, her legs parting slightly to reveal the dampness between her thighs. She was already aroused, and the sight of her barely concealed sex was almost too much for him to handle. Rachel looked him up and down, a predatory gleam in her eye as she began to unbuckle his pants. His cock sprang free, hard and eager, and Rachel took it in her hand, stroking it gently as she leaned in to whisper in his ear.

"You've come to the right place, John," she murmured, her breath hot against his neck. "I'm going to make all your dreams come true tonight."

John's eyes rolled back in his head as Rachel began to suck on the tip of his penis, her tongue swirling around the sensitive flesh. He could feel his body responding, his hips moving instinctively to the rhythm she set. Rachel's hand continued to work his shaft as she took more and more of him into her mouth, her teeth grazing gently against his skin.

With a gasp, Rachel released his cock from her mouth and stood up, pulling John with her. She led him upstairs, her naked body swaying in the candlelight, to a room that looked like it had been plucked from the pages of a lust-filled novel. The bed was massive, the sheets a dark, inviting shade of red, and there were an assortment of toys and restraints scattered around the room.

John watched, transfixed, as Rachel bent over the bed, her perfect ass beckoning him. She looked over her shoulder, her eyes meeting his, and he knew what she wanted. He stepped forward, his heart pounding in his chest, and positioned himself behind her. Rachel spread her legs wider, granting him full access to her slick, welcoming vagina.

He didn't need any further invitation. With one swift motion,

John pushed his cock into Rachel's tight opening, feeling her warmth envelop him. She moaned with pleasure, pushing back against him as he began to move. Rachel's walls tightened around him, and John knew that he was going to lose himself in her.

The room was filled with the sounds of skin slapping against skin, of Rachel's gasps and John's grunts of effort. Rachel's breasts bounced with every thrust, her nipples hard and erect, begging for his touch. He reached around her, squeezing and playing with them as he drove into her with increasing ferocity. Rachel's moans grew louder, her hips bucking back to meet him, urging him deeper, faster.

John could feel the tension building in his balls, his orgasm approaching like a freight train. Rachel sensed it too, reaching between her legs to rub her clit as they fucked. Her hand moved rapidly, her fingers dancing over her swollen bud, and she began to quiver with the beginnings of her climax.

The moment Rachel came, her pussy clamped down on John's cock like a vice, sending waves of pleasure through him. He couldn't hold back any longer, and with a roar, he exploded inside her, filling her with his hot, sticky cum. Rachel collapsed onto the bed, her body trembling with the aftershocks of pleasure, her pussy still spasming around John's cock.

They lay there for a moment, both of them panting and sweaty, their hearts racing in unison. Rachel rolled over onto her back, a satisfied smile playing on her lips. John pulled out of her, his cock glistening with their combined juices. Rachel took his hand and led him to the bed, where they lay side by side, their bodies still intertwined.

The night was far from over. Rachel had many more tricks up her sleeve, and John was eager to explore every inch of her willing body.

With a wink, Rachel got up from the bed and sauntered over to a chest of drawers, from which she produced a bottle of lube and a butt plug. John's eyes widened with excitement as she turned to face him, the plug twirling around her finger.

"Are you ready for the full experience?" Rachel asked, her voice a seductive purr.

John nodded, his cock already hardening at the prospect of new, uncharted territory. Rachel applied the lube generously to the plug before handing it to him. "Go ahead," she instructed, turning around and presenting her firm, round ass. "Prepare me."

John took the plug and lubed up his fingers, gently pushing one into Rachel's anus. She sighed with pleasure, pushing back against him as he worked his digit in and out. Rachel's body was so responsive, her muscles relaxing with each gentle probe. After a few minutes, John felt her body was ready, and he carefully inserted the plug, watching as Rachel's ass cheeks clenched around it.

Once the plug was in place, Rachel turned to face him, her eyes gleaming with excitement. "Now," she said, straddling him, "I want you to fuck me like you've never fucked anyone before."

John didn't need to be told twice. He grabbed Rachel's hips and pulled her down onto his cock, filling her pussy once again. Rachel moaned, the sensation of the plug in her ass combined with the feeling of John's cock in her pussy was overwhelming. They moved together, their bodies in perfect sync as Rachel rode him with an urgency that spoke of her desire to reach another climax.

John could feel Rachel's muscles tightening around the plug, her pussy clenching down on his cock. He knew she was close, and the thought of bringing her to another orgasm was too much to resist. He reached up, tweaking her nipples, as Rachel leaned forward, her breasts bouncing in his face.

With a final, deep thrust, John came, his cock pulsing as he filled Rachel up with his cum. Rachel's orgasm hit her like a wave, her body convulsing as she screamed out her pleasure. They stayed like that for a moment, Rachel's pussy contracting around his cock, both of them lost in the intensity of their shared release.

Finally, Rachel collapsed on top of him, their bodies sticky with sweat and cum. John wrapped his arms around her, feeling the aftershocks of their passion ripple through both of them. Rachel's breath was hot and heavy against his neck as she whispered, "Thank you for choosing me, John. I promise you, this is only the beginning."

The night stretched out before them, full of possibilities

and unspoken desires. Rachel's house had indeed become a sanctuary of carnality, and John had no intention of leaving anytime soon. He knew that with Rachel, every encounter would be an adventure, a chance to explore the darkest recesses of his sexual fantasies without judgment or inhibition.

As Rachel began to kiss her way down his body, John could already feel his cock stirring back to life, ready for the next round. He knew that he would leave this place a changed man, forever marked by the unbridled passion that Rachel had shared with him. But for now, he would simply revel in the feeling of her mouth on his skin, her tongue tracing the path that led to his swollen member.

Her warm, wet mouth enveloped him once more, and John sighed contentedly. The night was still young, and Rachel's appetite for pleasure seemed insatiable. He was more than happy to oblige, to lose himself in the depths of her mouth, her pussy, and her soul. This was a journey he had dreamed of, and now that he had taken the first step, he had no intention of turning back.

The Gym Instructor

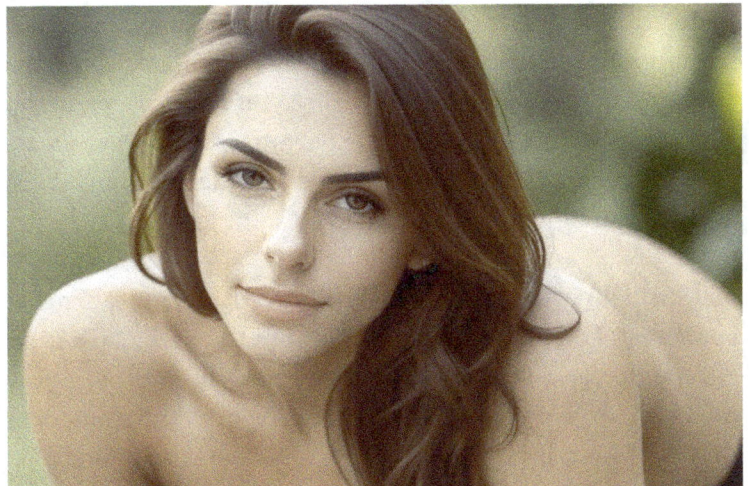

The gym was bustling with the usual mix of sweaty bodies and grunts of exertion, the faint smell of disinfectant doing its best to mask the more primal scents in the air. Amidst the clank of weights and rhythmic thump of the treadmills, Mark, the chiseled and charismatic gym instructor, had his eyes set on a new prize: a young, supple girl named Linda, whose shy demeanor and innocent glances had not gone unnoticed by his seasoned gaze. He knew she was a regular, always coming in right after her classes let out, trying to shed the baby fat that still clung to her in the most tantalizing of ways. She had the kind of body that made men like Mark salivate: soft in all the right places, with just a hint of the woman she would soon become.

As Linda stepped onto the elliptical machine, her tight leggings molded to her curvy figure, accentuating the gentle sway of her hips. Mark couldn't help but stare, his thoughts wandering to the treasures hidden beneath the fabric. He approached her, his confident stride and easy smile never failing to draw the attention of those around him. "Hey, you're new here, aren't you?" he asked, his voice a smooth purr that seemed to resonate through her very core. Linda blushed, her heart racing as she nodded, fumbling with the machine's settings.

"Let me help you with that," Mark offered, placing a firm yet gentle hand on her hip to guide her into the correct position. He couldn't resist letting his thumb graze the side of her ass, the fabric of her shorts stretching thinly over the roundness that begged to be squeezed. She gasped, a small sound that went unnoticed amidst the gym's cacophony. "There you go," he said, his eyes lingering on her body a moment longer than necessary before meeting her gaze. "If you ever need anything, don't hesitate to ask."

Their eyes locked for a brief second, a silent understanding passing between them. Mark could see the curiosity in hers, the way they dilated slightly, hinting at the desire that was beginning to stir within her. He knew she was ripe for the taking, and the thrill of the chase only made his blood pump

THE GYM INSTRUCTOR

faster.

The next day, as the gym's lights dimmed and the last patrons trickled out, Mark made his move. He'd been waiting for this moment, his cock thick and heavy with anticipation. He sauntered over to Linda, who was wiping down the yoga mats with a towel that was already soaked through with her own sweat. "Need some help with that?" he asked, his tone playful and suggestive. She looked up at him, her eyes wide and her cheeks flushed, clearly unprepared for his advances.

"I-I can manage," she stuttered, her voice betraying the excitement that was building in her belly. But Mark was insistent, his hand brushing against hers as he took the towel from her. His touch sent a jolt through her body, making her nipples harden into tight peaks against her sports bra. He leaned in, his breath hot on her ear. "Why don't you come to my office?" he murmured, his voice low and seductive. "I've got something I want to show you."

With trembling legs, Linda followed him to the small, private room at the back of the gym, her imagination running wild with what might happen next. She had never been with a man like Mark before, so sure of himself and oozing with sex appeal. The door clicked shut behind them, and she felt a thrill of apprehension mixed with desire. Mark turned to face her, his eyes raking over her body hungrily.

"You're even more beautiful than I thought," he said, his voice dropping to a whisper. "Let me show you what I can do for that body of yours." He reached out and traced a line from her neck down to her collarbone, his fingertips leaving a trail of fire in their wake. Linda's breath hitched, her eyes half-lidded with lust. He stepped closer, his hardness pressing against her stomach, making it clear what he wanted. And she wanted it too.

Without another word, Mark leaned in and captured Linda's lips in a searing kiss, his hands sliding down to cup her firm, round ass. She melted into him, her body responding instinctively to his touch. His tongue danced with hers, tasting the sweetness of her breath, and she felt a rush of wetness between her thighs. His hands grew bolder, caressing her hips before slipping around to the front and groping her breasts over her top. He pinched her nipples lightly, eliciting a soft moan that he swallowed eagerly.

Breaking the kiss, he pulled her shirt up over her head, revealing her heaving chest and the dampened cups of her sports bra. He took a moment to appreciate the sight, the pale pink fabric clinging to her erect nipples. With a swift motion, he unhooked her bra, freeing her breasts to bounce gently with her quickened breaths. He took one in his mouth, teasing the sensitive nub with his tongue, while his hand squeezed and molded the other. Linda's hands fumbled with the button of his gym shorts, desperate to feel the warmth of his skin against hers.

As she pushed his shorts down, his cock sprang free, thick and hard. She stared at it in awe, her hand tentatively reaching out to touch it. Mark groaned, the sensation of her soft, delicate hand on his shaft sending waves of pleasure through him. He guided her to her knees, and she took him in her mouth, her inexperience adding a certain innocence to the act that only served to drive him wilder. He watched as she bobbed her head, her eyes looking up at him with a mix of fear and excitement. He knew she was inexperienced, but her natural enthusiasm and eagerness to please made his knees wobble.

Finally, unable to resist any longer, Mark picked Linda up and laid her on the office desk, her legs spread wide for him. He pulled her shorts and panties down, exposing her bare, glistening pussy to the cool gym air. He took a moment to admire her, the way her folds glistened and begged for his attention. He leaned in and began to lick and kiss her inner thighs, moving closer and closer to her core. Linda's hips bucked, her breath coming in ragged gasps. When he finally reached her clit, she gasped, the sensation almost too much to bear. His tongue swirled and danced over her sensitive nub, bringing her closer and closer to the edge of orgasm.

He felt her body tighten, her muscles clenching around his tongue, and he knew she was close. With one final flick, he sent her over the edge, her moans of pleasure echoing through the empty gym. As her body shuddered with the aftershocks of her climax, Mark stood up and positioned himself between her legs. He rubbed the tip of his penis against her wetness, savoring the feeling of her slickness against his skin. With one swift thrust, he entered her, filling her completely. Linda's eyes went wide with a mix of pain and pleasure, her walls tightening around him. He began to move, slow at first, letting her adjust to the sensation, but gradually picking up the pace.

The sound of their bodies slapping together filled the room, a primal rhythm that seemed to resonate with the very air around them. Linda's moans grew louder, her nails digging into his back as he pounded into her. She wrapped her legs around his waist, pulling him deeper, urging him to give her more. Mark could feel the tension building in his own body, his orgasm approaching like a freight train. He reached down and began to rub her clit, feeling her body spasm around him as she reached the peak of her pleasure once again.

With a roar, Mark came, his hot seed filling her up. The feeling of her tight, wet pussy milking him was almost too much, and he had to hold onto the edge of the desk to keep from collapsing. They lay there, panting and sweaty, their bodies intertwined, for what felt like an eternity. It was a perfect moment of connection, a shared secret that bound them together in a way nothing else could.

The next day, Linda couldn't stop thinking about the steamy encounter she'd had with Mark. Her body felt alive with a newfound energy, and every time she passed the office where they'd fucked, her cheeks would flush with heat. She hadn't expected to see him again so soon, but there he was, standing by the water cooler, watching her approach with a knowing smile. "Ready for round two?" he whispered, his eyes glinting with mischief. Linda nodded, her pussy already throbbing with anticipation.

After her last class of the day, Mark picked her up and they headed straight to his apartment. As soon as the door closed behind them, they were on each other, kissing and groping with an urgency that spoke of unbridled lust. Mark led her to his bedroom, the walls adorned with posters of muscular men and women, the scent of his cologne heavy in the air. He pushed her onto the bed, his strong hands unbuttoning her blouse with practiced ease, exposing her ample breasts. He took one in his mouth, sucking hard on her nipple, while his hand found its way to her ankle, pulling off her shoe and sliding up her leg to tease her clit through her damp panties.

Linda moaned, arching her back, her body responding to his touch with a hunger she hadn't known she had. He slid her panties off, tossing them aside, and spread her legs wide. He took a moment to admire her, his eyes feasting on the pink, glistening flesh of her vagina. "So beautiful," he murmured, before leaning in to kiss her inner thighs, his breath hot against her skin. His tongue traced a line up to her clit, and she squirmed, unable to contain the whimpers that escaped her lips.

He began to lick her with a fervor that took her by surprise, his tongue swirling around her sensitive nub, dipping into her wetness, and then retreating only to tease her once more. Linda's hands tangled in his hair, urging him closer, her hips rising to meet his mouth. His lips closed around her clit, and he began to suck, hard and rhythmic, sending waves of pleasure crashing over her. She felt herself getting closer to the edge, her breath coming in ragged pants, her body coiled tightly like a spring ready to snap.

With a sudden jolt, she came, her back arching off the bed, her toes curling. Mark didn't stop, though, his tongue relentless as he drank in her sweet nectar, savoring every drop. Linda's orgasm washed over her, leaving her trembling and gasping for air. When he finally pulled away, she was a quivering mess, her body slick with sweat and desire.

"My turn," she whispered, her voice hoarse from the passionate cries she'd been unable to hold back. She pushed Mark onto his back and straddled him, her pussy still throbbing with the echoes of her climax. He was hard again, his cock standing tall and proud, begging for her touch. She took him in her mouth, eager to return the favor. Her inexperience showed a little as she took him deeper than she had the day before, gagging slightly, but she didn't care. The taste of him, the feeling of his hardness on her tongue, the way his body tensed beneath her, it was all so intoxicating.

Mark's hands found her breasts, playing with her nipples as she bobbed her head, taking him in and out of her mouth. His hips bucked, pushing himself deeper, and she could feel his excitement building. She swirled her tongue around the head of his penis, tracing the veins with her teeth before taking him all the way back in, her throat tightening around his shaft. She could feel his cock swell, and she knew he was close. With one final, deep suck, she felt him explode, his cum filling her mouth and spilling down her chin. She pulled back, a satisfied smile playing on her lips as she swallowed, savoring the taste of him.

They lay there for a moment, their bodies tangled together, basking in the afterglow of their passionate encounter. Then Mark sat up, his eyes gleaming with an intensity that made Linda's heart race all over again. "I've got a surprise for you," he said, his voice low and husky. He reached into his nightstand drawer and pulled out a blindfold and a bottle of lube. "Trust me," he murmured, placing the blindfold over her eyes and securing it gently.

The sudden darkness heightened her other senses, making every touch feel more intense. She felt him spread her legs wide again, his fingers sliding over her slick folds before pushing one inside her. She gasped, her body already begging for more. The sound of the lube being squirted onto his fingers made her heart pound in anticipation. And then she felt something new, something she'd never experienced before. A gentle pressure against her anus, and then the slow, steady intrusion of his lubricated digit.

The sensation was foreign and overwhelming, a mix of pleasure and pain that had her panting. He worked her gently, stretching her tight hole until she could feel his knuckles against her cheeks. She whimpered, her body adjusting to the new sensation, and then he added another finger, scissoring them inside her, preparing her for what was to come. Linda had never been so open, so vulnerable, and the thrill of it had her pussy gushing with excitement.

Finally, after what felt like an eternity of delicious torment, Mark removed his fingers and replaced them with the head of his cock. He took his time, pushing inch by inch into her virgin ass, his movements slow and steady. She could feel herself stretching to accommodate him, the pressure building until she thought she might split in two. But with each push, the pain melted away, replaced by a deep, all-consuming pleasure that had her writhing on the bed.

Once he was fully seated, he paused, giving her body time to adjust to the new sensation. Linda's breath was ragged, her pulse racing as she felt the fullness of his penis in her ass. He began to move, his strokes long and deliberate, each one sending shockwaves of pleasure through her body. She moaned, the sound muffled by the pillow she'd bitten into to stifle her cries.

As he fucked her ass, Mark leaned down and took one of her nipples into his mouth, sucking hard while his hand played with the other. Linda's hands clenched the bedsheets, her body tightening around him as she approached another orgasm. He could feel her sphincter pulsing against him, her body begging for release. "You're so tight," he murmured, his voice strained with his own effort to hold back. "So perfect."

Withdrawing slightly, Mark reached between them and began to rub her clit with his thumb. The added sensation was too much for Linda to handle, and she came with a scream, her body shaking uncontrollably. He watched her, his eyes dark with lust, as she rode out the waves of pleasure, her pussy clenching and unclenching around his thumb. When she finally stilled, he began to move again, his pace picking up, his strokes growing more urgent.

He knew he wouldn't last much longer, the feel of her tight ass gripping him too intense to resist. With one final, powerful thrust, Mark buried himself deep inside her, his cock pulsing as he came, filling her ass with his hot seed. They lay there, panting and spent, the only sound in the room the thump of their racing hearts.

The next day, Mark couldn't keep his hands off of Linda, constantly finding excuses to touch her and whisper dirty promises into her ear. The anticipation was driving her wild, and she found herself counting down the hours until she could be alone with him again. When they finally were, in the privacy of his apartment, they didn't waste any time. He led her to the bedroom, the same one where they'd shared their first night of passion, and she felt a thrill of excitement at the memories.

This time, however, Mark had something different in mind. He pushed her onto the bed, his eyes gleaming with a hunger that made her stomach flip. He stripped off his shirt, revealing the chiseled abs and broad chest that she hadn't had the chance to fully appreciate in the dim lighting of the gym. He leaned over her, his hard cock brushing against her stomach, and whispered, "I want to taste you again."

Without waiting for a response, he slithered down her body, his mouth leaving a trail of kisses on her skin. He parted her legs and dove between them, his tongue seeking out her swollen clit. Linda's body responded immediately, her hips rising to meet his eager mouth. He licked and sucked with a skill that left her breathless, his tongue delving deep into her wetness. She could feel herself getting closer and closer to the edge, her body tightening with each flick of his tongue.

Her moans grew louder as he worked her, his teeth gently grazing the sensitive flesh of her labia, his nose nuzzling against her pussy. And then, just as she was about to come, he stopped, his tongue retreating. Linda whined, desperate for release, but Mark had other plans. He climbed back up her body, his cock still hard and gleaming with pre-cum. He slid into her wet pussy, his movements slow and deliberate, filling her up completely.

The sensation of his thick cock in her was heavenly, and she wrapped her legs around his waist, urging him deeper. But Mark had a surprise for her. He reached down and began to rub her anus again, the lube making it easy for his fingers to slide in. Linda gasped as she felt him enter her ass with two fingers, the feeling of being filled in both holes sending her over the edge.

Her orgasm washed over her, more intense than any she'd ever felt before, her body convulsing with pleasure. Mark took advantage of her vulnerable state, sliding his cock out of her pussy and pressing the head against her tight, puckered asshole. Linda's eyes went wide with surprise, but she didn't resist. Instead, she pushed back, eager to experience the fullness she knew would come. He pushed in, her muscles giving way with a gasp, and began to fuck her ass in earnest, his strokes deep and powerful.

With each thrust, Linda felt her orgasm build again, her clit throbbing with every impact of his pelvis against her. He leaned down and captured her mouth in a deep, passionate kiss, their tongues tangling as their bodies moved in perfect harmony. She could feel his cock stretching her, filling her up in a way that was both painful and pleasurable. His hand found her clit once more, his thumb circling it with just the right amount of pressure, pushing her closer and closer to climax.

THE GYM INSTRUCTOR

As they moved together, Linda's mind was a whirlwind of sensations. The feel of his cock in her ass, the way his abs flexed with each thrust, the taste of him still lingering on her tongue—it was all too much. And when he finally reached down and began to suck on her clit, she shattered into a million pieces, her body bucking and spasming as she screamed out his name.

Mark felt Linda's body clench around his cock, her pussy pulsing with her orgasm. He couldn't hold back any longer, his own release imminent. He pulled out of her ass, and before she could protest, he slammed back into her pussy, the tightness of her ass making her pussy feel even tighter. He fucked her hard and fast, their bodies slapping together with a wet, carnally satisfying sound. Linda's moans grew louder, and he knew she was close again. He reached between her legs, his fingers finding her clit, and began to rub it with fervor.

Her breath hitched, her body tightening around him once more. He watched her, the way her breasts bounced with each thrust, the way her eyes rolled back in her head. And when she came again, screaming his name, it was his undoing. He let out a roar of pleasure, his cock erupting deep inside her, filling her up with his cum. They lay there, panting and sweaty, their bodies entwined, the evidence of their passion smeared between them.

When they finally parted, Linda felt a sense of euphoria wash over her. She had never experienced anything so raw, so intense, and she knew she was hooked. Mark pulled her into a tight embrace, his arms wrapping around her, holding her close as their breathing returned to normal. They lay there for a while, basking in the afterglow of their lovemaking, their hearts beating in sync.

As the reality of what had just transpired began to set in, Linda felt a mix of emotions: excitement, fear, and a deep, all-consuming need for more. She knew this was just the beginning, that there was so much more to explore with Mark. But she also knew that she couldn't let this become all-consuming. She had to keep her wits about her, maintain some semblance of control.

But as she felt his cock begin to stir again, pressing against her thigh, she realized that control might be harder to come by than she'd thought. "Again?" she whispered, her voice a mix of surprise and want. Mark chuckled, his hand sliding down to caress her still-sensitive clit. "Always," he murmured, before rolling her over and plunging back into her, ready to continue their erotic dance into the night.

Friend's daughter

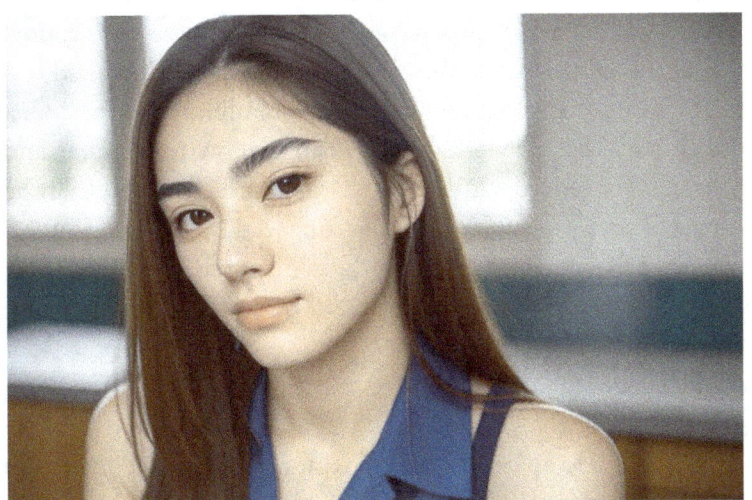

The sun had just set, casting a warm glow through the open curtains of Mark's living room, as he sat comfortably in his favorite armchair, sipping on a cold beer. The TV hummed in the background, but his thoughts were elsewhere. His best friend's daughter, Lily, had come to visit earlier that day, and she had been looking particularly… distressed. Mark had noticed the desperation in her eyes as she spoke of her financial troubles, and his mind began to wander to a place it hadn't been in years. Lily had always been a stunning young woman, with a figure that could make a saint sin. Her long, curly hair cascaded down her back, framing her heart-shaped face and full, pouting lips. Her eyes were a piercing blue that seemed to bore into his soul every time they met his gaze.

As the room grew dimmer, Mark couldn't shake the image of Lily from his thoughts. He recalled the way she had leaned in close to him when asking for help, her breasts pressing against his chest. The soft mounds of her cleavage had peeked out from her low-cut top, and he had felt a familiar stirring in his loins. It had been a while since he had been with a woman, and the sight of her youthful beauty was more tempting than he cared to admit. He knew it was wrong to think of her in such a way, but the devil on his shoulder whispered sweet nothings into his ear, suggesting a solution to both of their problems.

With a deep sigh, Mark decided to confront the situation head-on. He knew that Lily needed the money, and he had more than enough to spare. But he also knew that he could offer her something else entirely, something that would not only help her financially but also satisfy the burning desires he had kept hidden for so long. He took a deep breath, downed the rest of his beer, and stood up, heading towards her room.

Knocking softly on the door, he called out, "Lily, can I talk to you for a moment?" His voice was steady, but his heart hammered in his chest. There was a brief pause before the door creaked open, and Lily's worried face appeared in the gap. She looked up at him, her eyes wide with curiosity and a hint of fear. "What is it, Mark?" she asked, her voice quivering slightly. He took a moment to compose himself before speaking, his mind racing with thoughts of what was about to transpire.

"Look, I know you're in a tough spot with your finances," he began, trying to sound as casual as possible. "And I've been thinking… there might be another way I can help you out." Lily's eyebrows furrowed in confusion as she stepped aside, allowing him to enter her room. It was neat and orderly, a stark contrast to the tumultuous thoughts racing through her mind as she pondered what he could possibly mean.

Mark cleared his throat, his eyes lingering on her full, round breasts, which seemed to beg for his attention. "I know this is going to sound a bit… unconventional," he said, taking a seat on the edge of her bed. "But I have a proposition for you." Lily sat down next to him, her heart racing. "What kind of proposition?" she asked, her voice barely above a whisper.

With a heavy exhale, Mark turned to face her fully, his gaze dropping to her legs, which she had crossed demurely. "Well," he said, his voice thick with lust, "you see, I've noticed how… attractive you've become." He reached out and placed his hand on her thigh, his thumb brushing against the soft skin. "And I'm willing to help you out, if you're willing to help me out in return."

Lily's breath hitched as she felt the heat of his hand through her thin shorts. She knew what he was hinting at, and a part of her was both repulsed and intrigued. But desperation was a powerful motivator, and she couldn't deny the thrill that shot through her body at the thought of finally having her needs met. "What do you mean?" she asked, playing coy, her eyes never leaving his.

Mark took a deep breath and leaned in closer, his hand moving up to her hip. "I mean, if you give me what I want," he murmured, his voice low and gruff with desire, "I'll give you what you need." Lily's eyes searched his, a storm of emotions crossing her face—fear, anger, curiosity, and a spark of something else. Something that sent a thrill of anticipation through her body.

Her heart pounding in her chest, Lily swallowed hard and whispered, "What do you want?" Mark's eyes grew dark with lust as he leaned in even closer, his hand now caressing her waist. "I want you," he said simply. "Every inch of you. And I want you to want me too."

Lily felt the heat of his breath on her neck and a shiver ran down her spine. She knew this was wrong on so many levels, but the desperation was overwhelming. Her mind was a whirlwind of resistance and temptation. "I can't do that, Mark," she protested weakly, her body betraying her as she felt the beginnings of arousal pooling in her core. "It's not right."

He leaned back slightly, giving her room to breathe, his hand lingering on her hip. "You don't have to decide right now," he assured her, his voice soothing. "Just think about it. You can pay me back in any way you're comfortable with."

Taking a deep breath, Lily tried to calm the storm of emotions inside her. "What if I say no?" she challenged, her voice shaky.

Mark's expression grew serious. "Then I'll respect your decision," he said. "But I hope you'll consider it. I can make it worth your while." His hand slid up to her cheek, his thumb tracing her jawline. "You're so beautiful, Lily. And I've wanted you for so long."

The room grew thick with tension as they sat in silence, the only sound their ragged breaths. Lily's mind raced with thoughts of the consequences of giving in to Mark's proposal, but the allure of financial freedom was like a siren's call.

Finally, she spoke, her voice barely above a whisper. "What exactly are we talking about?" she asked, her eyes searching his for any sign of deceit. Mark leaned in closer, his voice low and seductive. "Whatever you're comfortable with," he said. "But I want to taste you, to feel you. And I know you want it too."

The words hung in the air between them like a physical force, and Lily felt a part of her resistance crumble. "But what if someone finds out?" she murmured, her hand trembling as she reached up to cover his.

He leaned in and kissed her, his lips gentle and coaxing. "It'll be our little secret," he promised, his voice a murmur against her mouth. "Just you and me."

Her resolve wavering, Lily found herself kissing him back, her body responding to the passion that had been building for so long. Mark's hand slid down her body, cupping her breast over her shirt. She gasped into his mouth, and he took the opportunity to deepen the kiss, his tongue exploring hers.

Breaking away, Mark took a moment to appreciate the sight of her flushed cheeks and swollen lips. "Let me show you how good it can be," he whispered, his hand sliding under her shirt to palm her bare flesh. "I'll take care of you, Lily."

Her eyes searched his, a silent plea for reassurance. Mark knew he had her, and he took a moment to savor the victory before leaning in to kiss her again, this time more urgently. Lily's hand slid down to his crotch, feeling the hardness beneath his pants. The last of her resistance crumbled as she realized that she was going to give in to the desire that had been simmering inside her for so long.

With trembling hands, she began to unbutton her top, revealing the creamy mounds of her breasts to his eager gaze. He groaned, his hand moving to cup one of her breasts, his thumb brushing against the pebbled nipple. The sensation sent a jolt of pleasure through her body, and she arched into his touch.

Mark wasted no time, his mouth descending to capture the sensitive peak. Lily gasped, her hands tangling in his hair as he suckled and teased her, his other hand sliding down to unbuckle his belt. His erection pressed against her thigh, hot and insistent, and she couldn't help but feel a thrill of excitement at the thought of what was to come.

Their kisses grew more frantic as they helped each other

undress, their bodies colliding with a need that could no longer be denied. Mark's hand found the dampness between her legs, and he groaned against her skin as he felt how ready she was for him. Lily's breath hitched as his fingers slid through her folds, teasing her clit before delving into her wetness. Despite her initial hesitation, she was unable to resist the overwhelming desire that had taken over her body.

"We can still stop," Mark murmured, his voice strained with restraint. He knew he had to give her an out, even though he desperately didn't want to. But Lily's response was to push his hand away, stand up, and pull her shorts and panties down in one swift motion. She stepped out of them, leaving herself completely exposed to his hungry gaze.

"I want this," she said, her voice firm despite the tremble in her legs. "But we have to be careful." Mark nodded, standing to meet her. He took a moment to drink in the sight of her naked body—the way her curves flowed like a sculptor's dream, the softness of her skin, the pinkness of her sex that beckoned to him like a forbidden fruit.

"We'll be careful," he agreed, his voice a low rumble. "But I need to know that you're sure." Lily met his gaze, her own desire clear in her eyes. "I'm sure," she whispered, taking a step towards him. "But I don't want to lose what we have."

He stepped closer, wrapping his arms around her waist and pulling her tight against his chest. "You won't," he promised, his erection pressing into her stomach. "This doesn't have to change anything." He kissed her again, his tongue delving into her mouth as his hands roamed her body. Lily moaned into the kiss, her fears momentarily forgotten as the heat between them grew.

Their bodies moved in sync as they explored each other, their hands and mouths everywhere. Mark's kisses trailed down her neck, across her collarbone, and down to her breasts, which he worshiped with the same intensity he had dreamed of for so long. Lily's own hands were busy, unbuckling his pants and freeing his erection. She wrapped her hand around it, stroking him gently as she felt it pulse in her grip.

"You're so hard," she murmured, her eyes wide with amazement. Mark chuckled, his breath hot against her skin. "You do that to me," he said, his voice thick with need. "Now, let me make you feel good." He knelt before her, pushing her legs apart. His eyes never left hers as he bent his head to kiss the inside of her thigh, moving closer and closer to the apex of her legs.

Lily's breath grew shallow as she felt his breath on her sex. "What are you doing?" she asked, her voice a mix of fear and anticipation. Mark looked up at her, a smoldering look in his eyes. "I'm going to taste you," he said, his voice a dark promise. "I've wanted to do this for so long."

He kissed the soft flesh of her inner thigh, moving closer to her center. Lily felt a jolt of pleasure run through her body, and she couldn't help but grip the bedcovers tightly. "But what if…" she started to protest, but he silenced her with a firm look.

"Shh," he soothed. "Just let go. Trust me." And with that, he lowered his mouth to her, his tongue sliding along her slit before plunging into her wetness. Lily's eyes rolled back in her head, a guttural moan escaping her lips. The sensation was overwhelming, and she knew that she had made the right decision.

For the next several minutes, Mark focused on her pleasure, his tongue and lips working in tandem to bring her closer and closer to the edge. Lily's resistance melted away under his expert touch, and she found herself bucking her hips against his face, begging for more.

As she climbed towards her peak, Mark slid a finger into her tight anus, the sensation sending her over the edge. She came hard, her body shuddering with the intensity of her orgasm. Mark didn't stop, his mouth working her clit until she was panting and begging for mercy.

When she had finally caught her breath, she looked down at him, his face glistening with her juices. "I can't believe I let you do that," she murmured, a hint of awe in her voice. Mark's eyes gleamed with satisfaction, but he knew that he had to proceed with caution. "Are you sure you want to continue?" he asked, his voice a gentle rumble.

Lily's eyes searched his, and for a moment, she seemed to waver. "I don't know," she whispered, her hand finding its way to her chest to cover her rapidly beating heart. "I just... it feels so wrong, but it also feels... right." He nodded, understanding the tumult of emotions she must be feeling. "Take your time," he said, standing and pulling her into his arms. "We don't have to rush into anything."

But the damage was done; the floodgates had been opened, and Lily's resistance was waning. She leaned into him, her soft curves pressing against his hard body. "What happens if we do this?" she asked, her voice small and scared. "What if my dad finds out?"

Mark kissed the top of her head, his arms tightening around her. "We'll be discreet," he assured her. "No one ever has to know." He knew that the temptation was too great, and he had to be the one to take the lead. He reached down and took her hand, guiding it back to his still-erect penis. "Feel how much I want you," he whispered, his voice thick with desire.

Her hand trembled as she touched him again, and Mark felt his own resolve waver. He wanted her so badly it was a physical ache. "Please," he said, his voice a desperate plea. "Let me make you feel good."

Her eyes searched his one last time before she nodded, a silent agreement passing between them. Mark knew that this was the point of no return, and he was ready to take the leap. He kissed her again, deeper this time, as he led her back to the bed.

Lily lay back, her legs spread, as Mark climbed on top of her. She felt his weight pressing her into the mattress, his erection nudging against her wetness. He paused, his eyes locked on hers. "Are you sure?" he asked again, giving her one last chance to back out.

Her answer was a soft moan as she reached up to kiss him again, her legs wrapping around his waist. He took that as the affirmation he needed and pushed into her, her warmth enveloping him like a glove. Lily's eyes went wide with the sensation, her nails digging into his back as he filled her completely.

He began to move, his hips pumping in a slow, steady rhythm that made her moan. Lily's body responded to him, her hips rising to meet his thrusts. Despite the wrongness of it all, she couldn't deny the pleasure he was giving her. "Oh, Mark," she whimpered, her voice lost in a sea of pleasure.

He kissed her neck, his teeth grazing her skin as he moved faster. She could feel him getting closer, his breath hot and ragged against her ear. "Tell me you like it," he growled, his voice demanding.

"I do," she gasped, the words torn from her chest. "I like it, Mark. I like it so much."

The room was filled with the sounds of their passion—the slap of skin on skin, the wet sounds of their coupling, and their mingled moans and gasps. Mark felt the familiar tightening in his balls, and he knew he was close. He reached between them, his thumb finding her clit again. Lily's back arched off the bed, her nails scratching at his skin as he applied just the right amount of pressure. Her cries grew louder, and he knew she was close too.

With a final, desperate thrust, he pushed her over the edge

again, her orgasm milking him as he spilled his seed inside her. They lay there, panting and trembling, their bodies slick with sweat. The air was heavy with the scent of sex, and the weight of their secret hung between them like a thick fog.

For a moment, neither of them spoke, lost in the aftermath of their passion. Then, Lily looked up at him, her eyes wide with a mix of confusion and need. "Was that...?" she started to ask, but Mark cut her off with a gentle kiss.

"It was perfect," he assured her, stroking her hair. "But we can't tell anyone, okay?" She nodded, her eyes searching his for the truth. "I know," she murmured. "It's just between us."

They lay there for a few more moments before Mark pulled out of her, the warmth of their combined releases coating his penis. He leaned over and kissed her again, his hand still caressing her body. "Thank you," he whispered, his voice hoarse with emotion. "Thank you for trusting me."

Lily's eyes searched his, the reality of what they had done finally setting in. "What now?" she asked, her voice small. "What happens next?"

Mark sighed, his hand tracing lazy circles on her stomach. "Now, we make sure you never have to worry about money again," he said, his voice firm. "And we keep this between us."

They lay in silence for a few more moments before Mark sat up, his erection still standing tall. "But first," he said, his voice thick with need, "I think we should clean up."

Lily watched as he stood and walked to the bathroom, his body still glistening from their encounter. She couldn't believe what she had just done, but she also couldn't deny the intense pleasure that he had given her. As he returned with a warm, wet washcloth, she realized that she didn't want it to end.

He gently cleaned her up, his touch surprisingly tender for someone who had just taken her so roughly. She felt a strange mix of emotions—shame, guilt, but also a burning desire to feel him inside her again. "Thank you," she murmured as he finished, her cheeks flushing with embarrassment.

He kissed her forehead and helped her sit up. "It's nothing," he said, his eyes lingering on her breasts. "But maybe next time, we can take it a bit slower, hmm?"

Lily nodded, the thought of a next time both thrilling and terrifying her. But she knew that she would agree to it, no matter what the cost. She was desperate for the release he had provided, and she didn't want to go back to the way things were before.

They both stood, their naked bodies a stark reminder of their newfound arrangement. "I'll get you the money tomorrow," Mark promised, pulling on his pants. "But for now, let's just get some rest."

Lily nodded again, her legs still shaking slightly. As he left the room, she couldn't help but wonder if she had just made the biggest mistake of her life—or the best decision she would ever make. Only time would tell.

Nurse

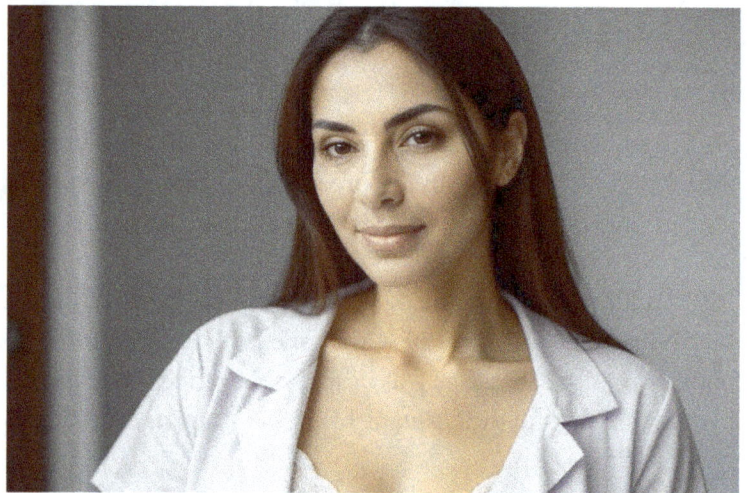

The sterile white walls of room 304 seemed to pulse with a secret, illicit energy that was palpable to the young nurse, Rachel, as she pushed the cart of supplies into the room. She had been working the night shift for nearly a year now, and she had grown quite accustomed to the quiet whispers of the hospital, the occasional moan of pain echoing down the hallways, and the gentle beeps of the monitors that pulled her into a rhythmic routine. However, there was something about tonight that was different—something that sent a delicious thrill down her spine and made her heart race just a bit faster than usual.

Her patient for the evening was a young man named Alex, with a chiseled jaw, piercing blue eyes, and a body that could have easily graced the cover of any fitness magazine. Rachel had noticed him the moment he was admitted—his muscular form strapped to the gurney, his broad chest rising and falling with the effort of his injuries. The doctor had assured her that while he was in no immediate danger, the severity of his fractures would require constant monitoring and care throughout the night. Little did Rachel know, she was about to embark on a night of pleasure that would not only break the monotony of her job but also push the boundaries of her own desires.

Alex lay in the hospital bed, his eyes fluttering open as Rachel approached. Despite the pain medication coursing through his veins, he couldn't help but appreciate the sight of her—her hair pulled back into a tight bun, her scrubs hugging the curves of her body in all the right places. Rachel's professional demeanor did little to mask the hint of mischief dancing in her eyes as she took his vital signs, her gentle touch lingering just a bit longer than necessary on his strong wrist. She noticed his gaze lingering on the ample cleavage peeking out from her V-neck top and felt a warmth spread through her body, hinting at the potential for a much more intimate interaction than either of them had planned.

The room was dimly lit, with only the soft glow of the medical monitors and the occasional flicker of the fluorescent lights above casting eerie shadows across the floor. Rachel's heart pounded in her chest as she took in the sight of Alex's bare chest, the bandages wrapping around his torso a stark contrast to the taut, unblemished skin of his biceps. She felt a sudden, overwhelming urge to touch him—to feel his warmth and strength beneath her fingertips. With a deep, steadying breath, she began to remove the bandages, her eyes never leaving his. His gaze was intense, holding hers with a promise of something more than just a medical examination.

The air grew thick with tension as Rachel revealed the extent of Alex's injuries. His left leg was encased in a cast up to his thigh, and his right arm was in a sling, leaving him vulnerable and exposed. Despite his weakened state, there was an undeniable attraction between them—a current that crackled and danced in the space between their bodies. Rachel's eyes trailed down to the bulge in his hospital-issued briefs, and she felt her cheeks flush with a mix of arousal and embarrassment. Alex's eyes followed hers, and he gave a low chuckle, his voice gruff with pain and desire.

"It seems like my body has other plans for the night," he said, his voice a seductive rumble. Rachel swallowed hard, her throat dry with anticipation. She knew that she should maintain a professional distance, but the allure of his virility was too much for her to resist.

With trembling hands, Rachel reached for the waistband of his briefs, her eyes never leaving his. She slowly began to lower them, revealing his swollen penis, which stood at attention despite his injuries. Alex's breath hitched as Rachel wrapped her hand around his shaft, her skin soft and cool against the heat of his arousal. He was thick and hard in her grip, and she felt a thrill of power at the way he reacted to her touch. Rachel licked her lips, her gaze locked on his, as she leaned in to take him in her mouth.

The first brush of her lips against his skin sent a jolt through his body, and he groaned, his hips rising slightly off the bed. Rachel took him deeper, her tongue swirling around his head as she took more of him into her mouth. Alex's hands found their way to her hair, tangling in the strands as he guided her movements, urging her to take more of him. She responded eagerly, her mouth sliding up and down his length, her cheeks hollowing with each suck. Rachel could feel the tension building in him, his muscles tensing and releasing as she worked her magic, bringing him closer and closer to the edge of ecstasy.

Alex's moans grew louder, and Rachel knew she had to be careful not to alert the other hospital staff. She reached up with her free hand to stroke his chest, feeling the rapid beat of his heart beneath her fingertips. His nipples hardened at her touch, and she pinched them lightly, eliciting a gasp from him. The sound of her mouth working him, the wetness of her tongue, the tightness of her throat—it was all too much for Alex to bear, and he knew he was close. Rachel could feel his cock pulsing in her mouth, and she increased her pace, her hand pumping in time with her sucks.

Finally, with a strangled cry, Alex came, his warm release filling Rachel's mouth. She swallowed eagerly, savoring the taste of him as she slowly pulled back. His eyes were squeezed shut, and his chest heaved with the exertion. Rachel sat up, her lips glistening, and wiped her mouth with the back of her hand, a satisfied smile playing at the corners of her mouth. She leaned over him, her ample breasts pressing against his chest, and whispered in his ear, "That's just the beginning, my dear patient."

Alex's eyes snapped open, and he met her gaze, his own smile matching hers in its wickedness. He reached up with his good arm, pulling her closer, and whispered back, "Then let's proceed with the next treatment, Nurse Rachel." Rachel felt a shiver of excitement run down her spine at the sound of her name on his lips. She knew that this was going to be a night she would never forget—a night where she would heal more than just his physical wounds.

With a nod of agreement, Rachel began to strip out of her scrubs, her own desire now taking over. She let her top fall to the floor, revealing her round, full boobs, the nipples already erect with need. Alex's eyes widened in appreciation, and he reached out with his good hand to cup one, his thumb brushing over the sensitive peak. Rachel moaned, her body responding to his touch as if it had been waiting for this moment for an eternity.

Her breasts were heavy and sensitive in his palm, and she could feel her pussy growing wet at the thought of what was to come. She reached down to untie her pants, letting them fall to her ankles, and stepped out of them, leaving her in just her panties. The scent of her arousal filled the room, mingling with the sterile aroma of the hospital. Rachel climbed onto the bed, straddling Alex's hips, her knees sinking into the mattress. His cock was already hardening again, and she could feel it pressing against her through the fabric of her underwear.

Leaning down, Rachel kissed him deeply, her tongue slipping into his mouth to dance with his. Her hand found its way between them, and she began to stroke his cock once more. Alex groaned into the kiss, his hands exploring her body, his fingers finding their way into the wetness between her legs. Rachel moaned into his mouth, grinding against his hand as he teased and rubbed her clit.

Without breaking the kiss, Rachel slid her panties aside, positioning herself over his erection. She felt the head of his penis nudge at her opening, and she took a deep breath before slowly lowering herself onto him. Alex filled her completely, stretching her walls in a way that was both painful and exquisite. Rachel moaned into his mouth as she began to ride him, her hips moving in a slow, sensuous rhythm that had them both panting with need.

Alex's hands roamed over Rachel's body, cupping her breasts, squeezing her ass, and gripping her hips as she moved above him. His thumbs found her clit, and he began to rub it in circles, sending waves of pleasure crashing through her. Rachel threw her head back, her hair cascading over her shoulders, as she took him deeper, her movements growing more urgent.

Their bodies moved together in perfect harmony, the only sounds in the room the slap of skin on skin and their muffled moans. Rachel could feel her orgasm building, her pussy clenching around Alex's cock, her breath coming in ragged gasps. He matched her rhythm, his hips rising to meet her as she took him in deeper with each stroke. The sensation was almost too much to handle, and Rachel felt like she was going to shatter into a million pieces.

Suddenly, she felt it—the peak of pleasure cresting over her, drowning her in a sea of sensation. She cried out, her body convulsing around Alex as she came. He followed her over the edge, his own release filling her up as he thrust one final time, his muscles tightening and his eyes squeezed shut in pure bliss. Rachel collapsed onto him, her chest heaving, her heart racing as the aftershocks of their union reverberated through her body.

For a moment, they lay there, panting and tangled together, the only sound of their mingled breaths. Rachel felt a warmth spread through her that had nothing to do with the exertion of their lovemaking. It was a warmth that came from deep within, a warmth that told her she had found something she didn't even know she was looking for.

Alex's hand found its way to her hair, stroking it softly as he whispered, "Thank you, Rachel." Rachel lifted her head, looking into his eyes, and smiled. "No, Alex," she murmured, her voice thick with emotion. "Thank you."

Their eyes locked, and Rachel felt a connection to Alex that she had never felt with anyone before. It was a connection that went beyond the physical, beyond the boundaries of their roles as patient and nurse. It was a connection of souls, two lost individuals finding solace in each other's arms amidst the cold, sterile hospital setting.

They lay there for a while longer, their bodies entwined, savoring the feeling of being alive, of being wanted, of being together. But all too soon, Rachel knew she had to get back to her duties, and had to pretend that the passionate encounter had never happened. With a sigh, she began to move off him, but Alex's arms tightened around her, keeping her close.

"Not yet," he whispered. "Let's enjoy this for just a little longer." Rachel nodded, nestling into his embrace. For now, she could ignore the beeping of the monitors and the ticking of the clock. For now, she could just be Rachel—the woman who had just experienced the most intense night of her life with a man she never thought she'd have the chance to be with.

Their bodies still humming with pleasure, Rachel and Alex held each other, their hearts beating as one. The line between duty and desire had been blurred, but in that moment, all that mattered was the connection they shared. As Rachel kissed him softly, she made a silent promise to herself that she would find a way to make this stolen night of passion a reality again and again.

The hospital was a place of healing, and Rachel had just discovered that sometimes, the most profound healing came from the most unexpected of places. With a smile, she pulled the blankets over their entwined forms, and for the rest of her shift, she would continue to nurse him back to health, both body and soul.

Lesbian Friend

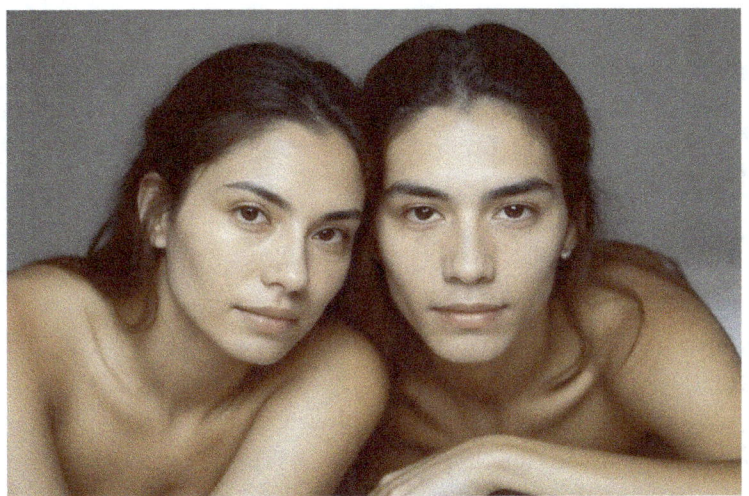

It had been a particularly dreary afternoon when Rachel found herself unable to resist the siren's call of her own desires any longer. Her mind had been wandering to the topic of intimacy for weeks, and the pent-up need for a physical connection was becoming unbearable. Rachel's thoughts kept drifting to her friend, Lena, who had always had an air of confidence and allure that Rachel found utterly captivating.

Though they had been friends for years, Rachel had never dared to cross the line she knew existed between them, fearing that her hidden feelings would ruin their friendship. However, the storm brewing within her grew more intense with each passing day, and she found herself fantasizing about Lena's soft touch and the warmth of her embrace.

One evening, as they lounged on Rachel's plush couch after a bottle of wine had loosened their inhibitions, Lena reached over and placed her hand gently on Rachel's thigh. Rachel's body responded almost involuntarily, her skin tingling and her breath catching in her throat. Lena's gaze was unmistakable; it held a promise of passion and exploration that Rachel could no longer ignore. She searched Lena's eyes for any sign of rejection, but found only desire mirrored in their depths. Rachel's heart raced as she made the decision to lean in, to kiss the woman who had been the star of so many of her secret fantasies. The moment their lips met, Rachel knew she had made the right choice. Lena's kiss was tender yet assertive, sending a shiver of excitement down Rachel's spine as their tongues danced together in a delicious dance of exploration.

Their kiss grew more heated as they fumbled with one another's clothes, eager to feel skin on skin. Rachel's hands slid over Lena's breasts, feeling the firmness of her erect nipples through the fabric of her shirt. Lena moaned softly against Rachel's mouth, her own hands unbuckling Rachel's belt and sliding down to caress her ass. Rachel shivered with pleasure at the sensation, her mind racing with the sudden reality of the situation. She had never been with a woman before, and the prospect of experiencing this kind of intimacy with Lena was both thrilling and terrifying. Yet, as Lena's expert touch grew bolder, Rachel found herself melting into the moment, eager to experience all that her friend had to offer.

Lena's hand traveled further down Rachel's body, her fingertips tracing the line of Rachel's panties. Rachel could feel the warmth of Lena's breath on her neck as she kissed and nibbled her way to Rachel's earlobe. Rachel gasped as Lena's fingers slipped beneath the fabric, teasing the wetness that had pooled between her thighs. The feeling of Lena's hand on her was electric, and Rachel arched into her touch. Lena chuckled softly, whispering, "You're so wet for me." Rachel could only nod, lost in the sensation as Lena began to stroke her clit with a gentle yet firm rhythm that had Rachel's legs shaking. Rachel had never been touched with such care and precision before, and she knew she was on the brink of something incredible.

Without breaking their kiss, Rachel managed to pull Lena's shirt over her head, revealing her firm, round boobs. Rachel had always admired them from afar, and now she had the chance to explore them up close. She took one in her mouth, flicking her tongue over the nipple as Lena gasped with pleasure. Rachel's hands roamed Lena's body, feeling the softness of her skin and the strength of her muscles. Rachel had always been a visual person, but the tactile experience was intoxicating. The way Lena's skin felt against her own, the way Lena's body moved and reacted to her touch, was unlike anything Rachel had ever experienced. Rachel felt a rush of power and desire as Lena's hands grew more insistent, pushing Rachel's pants down and off her legs. Rachel's pussy was bare and exposed to the cool air, but the chill was quickly forgotten as Lena's warm hand found its way back to her clit.

Rachel's hips bucked against Lena's hand as the pleasure grew more intense. She had never been so open and vulnerable with someone, but with Lena, it felt right. Rachel's hand slid down Lena's body, finding her way to her vagina. The heat was overwhelming, and Rachel could feel Lena's desire pulsing against her fingertips. Rachel slid one, then two fingers inside, feeling the wetness and warmth envelop them. Lena's moans grew louder, and Rachel felt a thrill of satisfaction knowing she was giving her friend pleasure. Rachel's thumb found Lena's clit and began to rub in sync with Lena's hand on her own. The room was filled with the sound of their breathing and the wet sounds of their arousal, their movements growing more frenzied as they brought each other closer to climax.

Suddenly, Lena's hand stopped, and Rachel's eyes flew open. Lena stood up, pulling Rachel to her feet. Rachel's eyes searched Lena's, but all she found was pure hunger. Lena led her to Rachel's bedroom, pushing her gently onto the bed. Rachel's heart was racing as she watched Lena strip off her own pants and underwear, revealing her bare sex. Rachel had never seen a woman's body so up close, so beautifully displayed, and she felt her own arousal spike. Lena crawled onto the bed, straddling Rachel's waist. Rachel could feel Lena's wetness against her stomach, and she knew that this was the moment she had been waiting for. Lena leaned down and kissed her again, her tongue delving deep as Rachel wrapped her arms around her friend, pulling her closer. Rachel knew that from this moment on, their friendship would never be the same, but she also knew that she wouldn't change a single thing. The only thing that mattered was the passionate embrace they were sharing, the feeling of Lena's body on top of hers, and the promise of the unexplored pleasures that lay ahead.

A Party Invitation

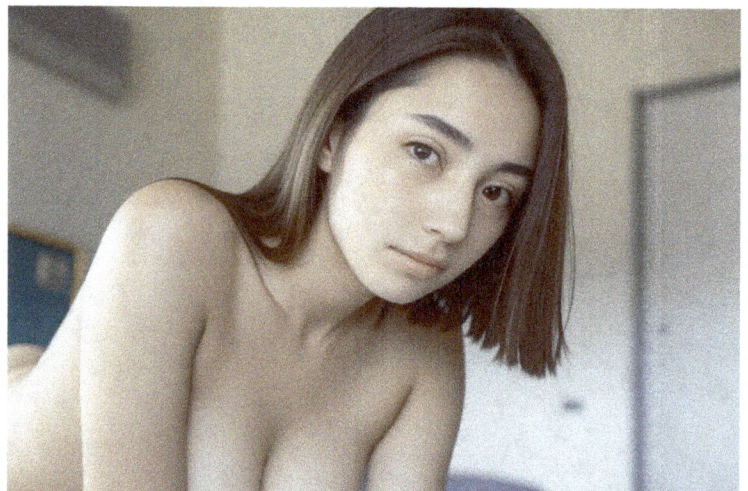

Luna, a fresh-faced college sophomore with a penchant for adventure, found herself in the throes of an unexpected evening as she stepped into the dimly lit party venue. The rhythmic bass of the music vibrated through her body, setting the stage for a night that would etch itself into her memory with the indelible ink of a wild tattoo. Her heart fluttered with a mix of excitement and trepidation as

A PARTY INVITATION

she scanned the room, her eyes adjusting to the kaleidoscope of colors from the strobing lights. She had been invited by a casual acquaintance, a guy from one of her classes named Alex, and she couldn't help but feel a thrill of anticipation at the prospect of what the night might hold.

Her eyes locked onto Alex, who was already several drinks deep, surrounded by a gaggle of his friends. He spotted her, his smile broadening, and gestured her over with a wave of his hand. She made her way through the sea of bodies, her hips swaying to the beat of the music. Luna was a stunner, with long raven hair cascading down her back and a figure that seemed sculpted by the hands of a divine artist. Her tight dress clung to her curves like a second skin, leaving little to the imagination. The heat from the room seemed to intensify with every step she took towards him, her heart thumping a seductive rhythm in her chest.

Alex, a tall, athletic young man with a boyish charm, pulled her into the circle and handed her a drink. "Luna, this is the crew," he said, slurring his words slightly. She nodded and smiled politely at each introduction, sipping on the sweet concoction that burned a fiery path down her throat. The party was already in full swing, the air thick with the scent of alcohol and pheromones. As the night progressed, the drinks flowed freely, and the conversations grew more hushed and intimate.

The party was a cacophony of laughter, music, and whispered secrets. Luna, feeling the warm embrace of the alcohol, allowed herself to let go of her inhibitions. Her cheeks flushed, she danced with an abandon that was unfamiliar yet exhilarating.

Alex watched her, his eyes dark with desire as she moved her body in time with the music. It was as if she were putting on a show just for him, and he was the lucky recipient of her performance.

Alex took her hand and led her away from the dance floor, through the throb of the party and into a quieter corner of the house. They stumbled into a bedroom, the door closing with an ominous click behind them. The room spun for a moment as the music faded into the background, leaving them in a cocoon of anticipation. He leaned in, whispering sweet nothings into her ear as his hand slid up her thigh, brushing against the lace of her panties. Luna's breath hitched, a shiver of excitement coursing through her. She had wanted this, hadn't she? To feel alive, to explore the boundaries of desire that lay just beneath the surface of everyday life.

With a gentle push, he guided her onto the bed, his eyes never leaving hers. She watched as he unbuttoned his shirt, revealing a chiseled chest that made her mouth water. The room was spinning now, the lines between reality and fantasy blurring like watercolor on wet paper. She felt his warm breath against her neck as he kissed her, his teeth grazing her sensitive skin. The sensation sent bolts of pleasure straight to her core, and she moaned, arching into him. His hands explored her body with a hunger that matched her own, unhooking her bra with ease and cupping her ample breasts.

Her nipples hardened under his touch, begging for more, and he obliged, sucking and nipping at them until she was a writhing mess of pleasure beneath him. Luna's hands found the hem of her dress, eagerly pulling it up and over her head, leaving her in nothing but her lacy lingerie. Alex took his time, tracing the lines of her body with his fingers before his mouth followed the path he'd laid. He kissed and licked her stomach, his tongue swirling around her navel before moving lower.

When he reached the apex of her thighs, she spread her legs wider, inviting him in. Alex's eyes lit up with lust as he took in the sight of Luna's drenched panties. He slid them down her legs with the grace of a seducer, exposing her bare pussy to the cool air of the room. He buried his face between her thighs, inhaling her sweet scent before diving in with his tongue. Luna's back arched off the bed as he licked and sucked at her clit, bringing her closer and closer to the brink of orgasm. She could feel her walls tightening around his tongue, her breaths coming in ragged gasps. His teeth grazed her sensitive folds, sending electric currents through her body. She reached down to tangle her fingers in his hair, urging him on as the pleasure mounted.

Her hips bucked as the first wave of climax hit her, her legs trembling uncontrollably. Alex didn't stop, continuing to pleasure her with a fervor that left her breathless. Each stroke of his tongue sent her spiraling higher until she was lost in the abyss of ecstasy. When she finally came down from the peak, her body limp and sated, she looked up at him with a mix of awe and need. He grinned, the corners of his eyes crinkling in satisfaction before he moved to kiss her, sharing her taste. She wrapped her arms around his neck, pulling him closer, their kisses growing more feverish as their bodies aligned.

His erection pressed against her, and she could feel the heat of him through his pants. With a deft move, she unbuckled his belt, her nimble fingers making quick work of his zipper. She reached inside and grasped his hard cock, giving it a squeeze that made him groan against her lips. He was thick and velvety, his skin hot to the touch. Luna couldn't wait to feel him inside her, to lose herself in the throes of passion once more.

Alex pushed her onto her back, his hands exploring her body with renewed vigor. He kissed her neck, sucking and biting gently before moving down to her breasts. He took a nipple in his mouth, teasing and flicking it with his tongue as he slid a finger into her wetness. Luna's moans grew louder, her hips rising to meet his touch. He added another finger, pumping them in and out as he twirled his thumb around her clit. The sensation was overwhelming, a crescendo of pleasure building within her once again.

Her legs spread wider, and she could feel the heat of his cock against her thigh as he slid his hand down her body. He paused for a moment, his finger lingering at her back door, before pushing gently against it. Luna gasped, the sensation foreign but incredibly arousing. He looked up at her, seeking permission, and she nodded eagerly, her cheeks flushed with excitement. He lubricated her ass with her own juices, sliding his finger in and out as he continued to work her pussy with the other hand. The dual sensation was too much, and she came again, her body shaking with the force of her orgasm.

With a groan, Alex positioned himself between her legs, the tip of his cock brushing against her entrance. He looked into her eyes, his own filled with a raw need that mirrored her own. "Are you sure?" he whispered, his voice thick with desire. "Yes," she breathed, her voice barely audible. He pushed inside her slowly, inch by inch, filling her up until she was stretched to the brink of discomfort. The feeling was intense, a mix of pain and pleasure that had her clutching the bed sheets. He began to move, his hips pumping in a steady rhythm that grew faster and harder with every thrust.

The sound of their bodies slapping together filled the room, mingling with her cries of ecstasy. She could feel every ridge and vein of his cock as it plunged into her, her pussy gripping him tightly. He reached down to tweak her nipples, sending shockwaves of pleasure through her body. The room was a blur of colors and sounds, the only thing clear in her mind the feel of Alex claiming her.

Luna's legs wrapped around his waist, pulling him deeper, urging him to take her even harder. Her hands slid down his back, her nails digging into his skin, leaving a trail of red marks in their wake. She could feel her climax building again, a pressure that was both intense and delicious. Alex sensed her urgency and picked up the pace, his strokes becoming more urgent as he approached his own peak.

Her walls tightened around him, and she screamed his name as she came, her body convulsing in pleasure. He followed her over the edge, his cock pulsing inside her as he filled her with his warmth. They lay there for a moment, their chests heaving in unison, their bodies slick with sweat. The room felt alive with the energy of their shared release.

Alex kissed her gently, his hand caressing her cheek as he withdrew from her. He looked into her eyes, searching for any sign of regret. But all he saw was satisfaction, a spark that told him she had enjoyed every moment of their encounter. He leaned down to whisper in her ear, "You're incredible, Luna."

Her eyes fluttered closed at the sound of her name on his lips. In that moment, she felt wanted, desired, and powerful. She knew this was just the beginning of a night that would be etched into her memory for a long time to come, a story she'd replay in her mind during quiet moments of solitude, a secret thrill that was theirs alone.

Met In Club

The pulsating lights of the crowded club illuminated a sea of gyrating bodies, the bass of the music vibrating through the very air itself. It was a cacophony of senses, a veritable feast for the eyes and the ears. In the midst of this chaotic symphony, a girl caught my eye. Her name was Charlotte, a vision in a tight, crimson dress that clung to her curves like a second skin. She had long, auburn hair that cascaded over her shoulders, framing a face that was an exquisite blend of innocence and sensuality. Her green eyes sparkled with mischief as she danced, and the way she moved her hips was nothing short of hypnotic.

I approached her with a drink in hand, my heart racing like a rabbit's in a hunter's sight. She looked up at me with a smile that could melt the polar ice caps. We didn't say much; the thundering music didn't allow for conversation. But our bodies spoke a language of their own. Her eyes locked onto mine, and I knew she felt the same primal pull that I did. The air between us was thick with desire, and I could almost taste the sweetness of her breath as we danced closer, our bodies pressing together in time with the beat.

Our dance grew increasingly intimate, her hands roaming over my chest as we moved in a passionate embrace. I could feel her hot breath on my neck, sending shivers down my spine. The music grew louder, the lights flashed faster, and the room around us melted away. It was just the two of us, lost in the throes of our own little world. And at that moment, the decision was made. We had to have each other.

With a nod, we slipped away from the dance floor, our hands entwined. The bathroom was the only place we could find a semblance of privacy. She led the way, her hips swaying seductively with every step. The anticipation was almost unbearable as we stepped into the dimly lit stall and locked the door behind us. The sound of the club was muted now, replaced by the sound of our own ragged breaths.

In the cramped space of the bathroom stall, the tension between us was palpable, our bodies a mere whisper apart. My hand found hers and brought it to the front of my jeans, where she could feel my throbbing erection. Charlotte's eyes widened with excitement, and she leaned in to kiss me, our tongues dancing together as if they had been separated by a lifetime of longing. The taste of her was intoxicating, a blend of mint and lust that fueled the fire within me. Her hand traced the outline of my cock through the fabric, her touch sending bolts of pleasure shooting through my veins. I couldn't wait any longer.

With a swift movement, I lifted her onto the sink, her legs wrapping around my waist. She moaned into my mouth as I ground against her, the friction of our bodies driving us both wild. I reached under her dress and found her wet panties, the scent of her arousal flooding my senses. I slid them aside, revealing her glistening pussy, begging for attention. My fingers found her clit and began to circle it gently as she bucked against my hand, her breath coming in gasps.

Her hand found its way to the zipper of my pants, and she freed my cock with a sense of urgency. She looked down at it with a mix of awe and hunger, her eyes never leaving mine as she wrapped her soft, delicate hand around the shaft. I groaned, the feel of her touch almost too much to handle. She stroked me slowly at first, her eyes fluttering closed with pleasure as she felt my hardness in her grasp. I reached between her legs and slid two fingers inside her, feeling the warm embrace of her vagina. She was tight and wet, and her moans grew louder as I curled my fingers and found that magical spot that made her legs quiver.

As we fucked in that tiny bathroom stall, the sound of the club outside became nothing but a distant murmur. All that mattered was the friction of skin on skin, the slickness of our desire, and the rhythm of our hips crashing together. I felt her climax building, her pussy tightening around my fingers, and I knew she was close. I leaned in and whispered her name, "Charlotte," in her ear, and she responded by biting down on my shoulder, her nails digging into my back. She came with a muffled scream, her body convulsing with pleasure.

Her climax only served to drive me further into a frenzy. I pulled her closer, the head of my cock brushing against her wet folds. She nodded, her eyes glazed with lust, and I slammed into her, filling her completely. The sound of our bodies slapping together echoed in the stall as I fucked her with an animalistic need that seemed to consume us both. She was so tight, so wet, and so incredibly responsive.

We didn't hold back, our hips moving in a primal dance that was as old as time itself. I felt my own orgasm building, and I knew it was going to be intense. With one final, powerful thrust, I came deep inside her, her walls contracting around me as I emptied myself. We held onto each other for a moment, our breaths mingling as we both came down from our shared high.

We straightened our clothes, and she gave me a wink before we exited the stall. The club was still in full swing, but we had found our own secret paradise. We stumbled back into the fray, the taste of each other still lingering on our lips, the promise of what was to come later at my place a sweet, heady scent that clung to us like a fine perfume. The night was young, and our appetites were far from sated.

Back at my place, the air was electric. We didn't bother with small talk or pleasantries. The hunger between us was too great to ignore. We tore at each other's clothes like animals in heat, desperate to feel every inch of bare flesh. I lifted her onto the kitchen counter, her legs parted wide as I feasted on her pussy. The sweetness of her arousal filled my mouth, and her moans grew louder with each swipe of my tongue.

Charlotte's hands were in my hair, pulling me closer, guiding me deeper as she rode my face. I could feel her body tense, her breath hitching in her throat as she approached another climax. And when she came, her thighs trembled around my head, and her nails dug into my scalp, leaving a trail of pleasure-pain that only served to drive me on. I licked and sucked, savoring every drop of her juices, until she pushed me away, gasping for air.

Standing up, I kissed her deeply, our tongues dancing together as I carried her to the bedroom. She was light in my arms, a goddess of desire that I couldn't wait to worship. Once there, we tumbled onto the bed, our limbs entwined as we continued to explore each other's bodies. Her breasts were perfect, her nipples hard and sensitive to the touch. I sucked and bit at them, drawing gasps from her as she writhed beneath me.

Her hand found its way back to my cock, stroking it gently as she took it into her mouth. The warmth and wetness were almost too much to handle, and I watched in amazement as she took me deep, her eyes never leaving mine. The way her cheeks hollowed as she sucked, the little moan she gave with every bob of her head - it was a symphony of pleasure that I never wanted to end.

But I knew there was more to come. I rolled her onto her back and slid down her body, my tongue tracing the path my hands had taken earlier. I licked her navel, her hips, and finally reached her pussy again, eager to taste her once more. She was even wetter now, and the scent of our combined desire filled the air. I lapped at her, feeling her squirm and buck beneath me. Her hands gripped the bed sheets, her legs quivering as I worked my magic on her clit.

And when she came, it was like watching a star explode. Her whole body tightened, her back arched off the bed, and she screamed my name. It was a sound that I knew I would never forget, a declaration of ecstasy that seemed to shake the very foundations of the room.

Our night grew wilder, our desires unbridled. I whispered into her ear, asking if she was ready for more. She nodded, her eyes dark with lust. I reached into the bedside drawer and pulled out a tube of lubricant and a condom. She watched, her breath shallow, as I rolled it onto my cock. Then, with a gentle nudge, I began to push into her ass, her tightness giving way to the pressure.

The sensation was unlike anything I had ever felt before. She was so tight, so warm, and she moaned in a way that sent shivers down my spine. I took it slow at first, easing into her inch by inch, making sure she was comfortable. But as she grew more accustomed to the feeling, she began to push back, her body begging for more.

I picked up the pace, my cock sliding in and out of her ass with a smoothness that seemed almost unnatural. The slickness of the lube combined with her own arousal made it feel like I was fucking a warm, wet velvet glove. Her nails dug into my shoulders, her body trembling with every thrust. I knew she was close again, and the thought of making her come in such a forbidden way was almost too much to bear.

With a final, powerful push, she did just that, her body convulsing around me as she screamed my name. It was all I could take, and I followed her over the edge, my cock pulsing deep inside her as I filled the condom with my cum. We lay there, panting and sweating, our bodies a tangle of limbs, the aftershocks of pleasure still echoing through us both.

After a moment, she looked up at me, her green eyes gleaming with satisfaction. "Take me again," she breathed, and I couldn't refuse her. We switched positions, her now straddling me, her ass still slick with lube. She took me in her hand and guided me back to her pussy, the feeling of her wetness making me even harder than before.

The fourth paragraph should be an escalation of their sexual encounter, possibly including power play.

With a wicked grin, Charlotte leaned down and whispered, "Let me be in charge." I nodded, the thrill of submission sending a fresh wave of arousal through me. She slid down onto my cock, her pussy swallowing me whole, and began to ride me. Her movements were deliberate and sensual, each roll of her hips sending waves of pleasure through my body.

As she rode me, her breasts bouncing with each bounce, she reached behind and grabbed my wrists, pulling them above my head. "Keep your hands here," she ordered, a playful but firm tone in her voice. I obeyed, the feeling of her in control making me harder than I ever thought possible. She leaned down and bit my lip, her teeth grazing against the tender flesh as she picked up the pace.

Our bodies moved as one, her hips grinding against mine as

she took her pleasure. I could feel the beginnings of another orgasm building, but I held back, not wanting it to end just yet. She sensed it too, her eyes never leaving mine as she leaned in closer, her breath hot against my ear. "Cum for me," she demanded, and with that, I lost all control.

The climax hit me like a freight train, my body arching off the bed as I filled her with everything I had. She didn't stop, though, riding me through the storm of pleasure until I was spent, my cock twitching with aftershocks. Only then did she allow herself to come, her muscles clenching around me as she threw her head back and screamed my name.

We lay there, tangled in the sheets, our hearts racing in tandem. The night was still young, but the fire between us had reached a crescendo. We had pushed each other to heights we had never known, explored every inch of each other's bodies. And as we lay in the quiet aftermath, I knew that this was just the beginning of a wild, erotic adventure that would burn brightly for hours to come.

Aunt Ana

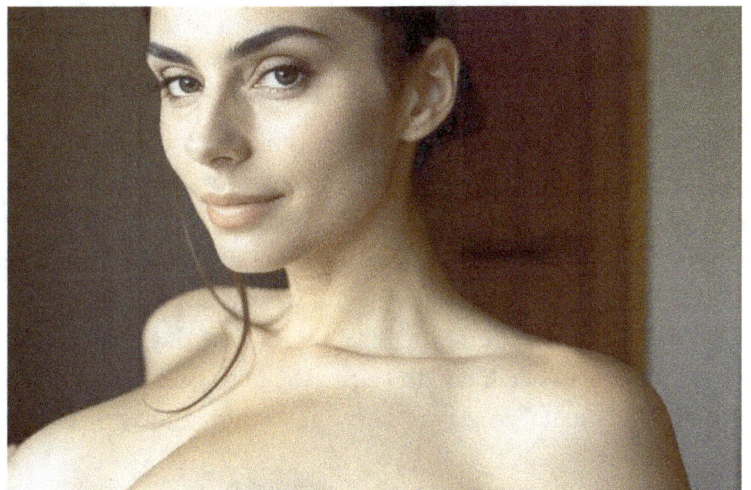

Ana, a stunning brunette with piercing green eyes and a smile that could light up any room, had arrived unannounced at the young boy's house. She was a long-lost friend of his mother, and their reunion was filled with warm embraces and nostalgic laughter. Little did she know, the boy, a lanky teenager with a mischievous glint in his eye, had been secretly harboring a deep-rooted lust for her ever since he had first set eyes on her in a family photograph.

The first night of her stay, Ana settled into the guest room, her heart racing with excitement for the days ahead. The boy, whose name was Alex, lay in his bed, listening to the faint sound of her unpacking her suitcase. He could feel the heat building in his loins as he thought about the woman who had just walked into his life, so close yet so untouchable. With each rustle of fabric, his imagination painted a more vivid picture of her undressing, revealing the supple curves that had been hidden under her clothes all along.

The following morning, Ana emerged from her room wearing a sheer, white nightgown that clung to her voluptuous figure. Alex couldn't help but stare, his eyes lingering on the tantalizing shadow of her nipples pressing against the flimsy fabric. She caught his gaze and offered a playful wink, oblivious to the fire she was stoking within him. Throughout the day, the tension grew thick between them, the air in the house charged with an undeniable sexual energy that neither could ignore.

As the sun dipped below the horizon and the house grew quiet, Alex decided to take a chance. He tiptoed to Ana's door, his heart hammering in his chest. He slowly turned the knob, pushing it open just enough to peer inside. The sight that greeted him was more than he could have ever hoped for: Ana lay on the bed, her nightgown hiked up to expose her shaven mound, one hand idly toying with her clit while the other squeezed her full, round breasts. She moaned softly, lost in a world of pleasure, unaware of the hungry eyes watching her from the shadows.

Alex's cock grew rock-hard as he took in the sight of her spread legs, her wet pussy glistening in the soft light. He knew he had to have her, to feel her warmth and taste her sweetness. Summoning his courage, he stepped into the room and closed the door behind him, the click echoing through the stillness of the night.

"Ana," he whispered, his voice barely above a breath. She looked up, surprised but not alarmed, her eyes glazed over with arousal. He took a deep breath and began his seduction, his words flowing like a sweet, seductive melody. "You're so beautiful. I've thought about you…touching you…for so long. I know this is wrong, but I can't help myself."

Ana sat up, the sheets pooling around her waist, exposing her perfect ass. She looked at him with a mix of curiosity and hunger. "Alex," she murmured, "you're just a boy."

"But I'm not," he insisted, taking a step closer, "I'm a man. And I want to show you how much." He reached out, his hand brushing against her thigh. "Let me make you feel good."

Her eyes searched his, looking for any sign of doubt or hesitation. Finding none, she bit her bottom lip and spoke in a low, sultry voice. "What makes you think I don't feel good already?"

Alex swallowed hard, his pulse racing as he leaned in closer. "I want to make sure," he murmured, his hand moving up to cup one of her breasts. "To give you something to remember."

Her breath hitched as his thumb brushed over her erect nipple. "What if someone hears us?" she asked, her voice a soft challenge.

"They won't," he assured her, his voice husky with need. "Let's just enjoy this moment together."

With a sly smile, she leaned back on the pillows, giving him the invitation he had been craving. His heart pounded as he slid onto the bed, his body pressed against hers, feeling the heat of her skin against his own. He kissed her neck, moving down to her collarbone, his hands exploring her body with a gentle yet insistent touch. Her moans grew louder as he worked his way down, finally reaching her swollen clit. He took it between his thumb and forefinger, gently rubbing in circles as she arched her back.

Her eyes rolled back in her head as he replaced his hand with his mouth, his tongue swirling around her clit as she squirmed beneath him. She reached down to grab his hair, urging him closer, her legs spread wider. He eagerly obliged, his tongue delving into her wetness, tasting her sweetness, feeling her body tighten around him. Her hips began to rock in rhythm with his movements, and he knew she was close.

"Oh, Alex," she gasped, "you're so…so…good."

Encouraged by her response, he slipped a finger inside her, feeling her walls clench around him as he continued to lick and suck her clit. Her moans grew more frantic, and he knew she was about to come. He pushed a second finger in, pumping them in and out as she bucked against him, her orgasm washing over her like a tidal wave.

As her tremors subsided, he looked up at her flushed face, feeling a sense of pride and lust. She was his for the taking, and he was going to make her scream with pleasure all night long.

Ana's eyes met his, her pupils dilated with desire. "Now," she panted, "now it's your turn." She reached down to unbuckle his belt, her hand shaking with anticipation.

Alex's cock sprang free, thick and hard. She wrapped her hand around it, her grip firm and sure, stroking him from base to tip. He threw his head back with a groan, his eyes squeezed shut.

"Suck it," he demanded, his voice thick with need. "Please, I need to feel your mouth on me."

Without a word, she leaned forward, her hot breath ghosting over his sensitive flesh before she took him in her mouth. The sensation was exquisite, her wetness enveloping him, her tongue swirling around the head of his cock. He gripped the sheets, fighting the urge to thrust deeper, to lose control.

But he had other plans for her. He wanted to make her feel just as good as she had made him feel. With a low growl, he pushed her onto her back, climbing over her. "Now,"

Alex whispered, "now I'll show you how much I've learned." He spread her legs wide and took in the beauty of her sex, his eyes feasting on her pink folds and glistening wetness. He leaned in, his cock throbbing, and kissed her inner thighs, moving closer to her core with every peck. He felt her legs tense up and knew she was eager for more.

As he licked her pussy, he inserted a finger into her tight ass, feeling the muscles clench around him. He heard her gasp, her body jolting in surprise, and he knew he had found a new spot to explore. He slid his finger in and out, lubricating it with her juices, all the while his tongue danced over her clit, bringing her to the edge once more.

"Oh, baby," she moaned, her nails digging into his shoulders. "That's…that's so good."

The praise spurred him on, and he added a second finger, preparing her for what was to come. She bucked against him, her breaths coming in ragged pants. He could feel her tightening around him, the anticipation of his cock filling her up.

Finally, unable to wait any longer, Alex lined his cock up with her dripping entrance and pushed inside, feeling her slick walls stretch to accommodate him. Ana let out a low groan, her eyes snapping open to look at him. He paused for a moment, watching her face, memorizing every twitch of her features as he filled her completely.

And then he began to move, his hips rolling in a steady, deep rhythm. She matched his pace, lifting her own hips to meet him, urging him deeper with every thrust. The bed squeaked in protest beneath them, but they paid it no mind. They were lost in their own world, a place where only pleasure mattered.

He reached down to play with her clit as he fucked her, feeling her tighten around him with every stroke. Her moans grew louder, more demanding, and he knew she was close to another orgasm. He picked up the pace, his own need growing more urgent with every passing second.

"I'm gonna come," she gasped, her voice strained with passion. "Fuck me harder, Alex. Make me come."

He obeyed, his thrusts growing more erratic as his own climax approached. He felt it building in his balls, the pressure growing until it was unbearable. And then, with a roar, he released it all inside her, filling her with his seed as she clenched around him, her body shaking with the force of her orgasm.

Their bodies remained intertwined for several moments, both of them panting and trying to catch their breath. He kissed her neck, her breasts, her lips, savoring the taste of her sweetness. "That," he murmured, "was amazing."

Ana could only nod, a blissful smile playing on her lips. She had never felt so alive, so wanted. And she had a feeling this was just the beginning of a very memorable visit.

They broke apart, both needing to catch their breath. Alex's cock slid out of her with a wet sound, leaving her feeling empty yet satisfied. She watched as he lay beside her, his chest rising and falling heavily, and she couldn't help but reach out to stroke his cheek. "You're something else," she murmured.

He grinned, his eyes sparkling with mischief. "I aim to please."

They lay there, tangled in the sheets, basking in the afterglow of their shared passion. But the night was still young, and there was so much more they hadn't explored.

With a sly look in his eyes, Alex began to kiss his way down her body again, his hands roaming over her curves as he went. He paused at her breasts, teasing the sensitive peaks until they were hard and pink. Then he moved further south, his tongue tracing a path down her stomach to the juncture of her thighs.

This time, he focused solely on her clit, flicking it rapidly as he pushed his fingers in and out of her tight hole. The sensation was almost too much for Ana to handle, and she began to moan and thrash beneath him. He felt her muscles clench around his digits, and he knew she was getting close again.

But before she could come, he pulled away, leaving her gasping. "Not yet," he whispered, his voice dark with intent. "I want you to feel me everywhere."

He climbed over her again, aligning his cock with her ass. He'd been dreaming of taking her there for months, and now the opportunity was finally here. He spit in his hand, using the saliva to lubricate her tight rosebud. He knew it would be tight, but he was eager to push through the initial discomfort and feel the ultimate connection.

Without warning, he pushed forward, the head of his cock breaching her tight sphincter. She let out a sharp cry, her body tensing. He paused, giving her a moment to adjust before he pushed further, inch by inch, until he was fully seated inside her. The feeling was indescribable, a mix of pain and pleasure that only served to make him harder.

Her nails dug into his back as he began to move, her moans turning into whimpers. He leaned down to kiss her, his teeth grazing her bottom lip as he picked up the pace. She wrapped her legs around his waist, urging him deeper, her body now accepting the intrusion with wanton abandon.

He reached down to play with her clit again, the dual sensations driving her wild. He felt her body begin to shake, her ass clamping down around his cock as she screamed his name, her orgasm ripping through her.

Alex couldn't hold out much longer. He felt the familiar tightening in his balls and knew he was going to come. He pulled out just in time, spurting his load onto her ass and back, marking her as his.

They collapsed onto the bed, exhausted and sated. They had crossed a line that could never be uncrossed, but in that moment, neither of them cared. All that mattered was the here and now, and the promise of what was still to come.

Ana rolled over onto her side, her breaths coming in shallow pants. Alex pulled her into his arms, his cock still semi-hard against her thigh. "I want more," he murmured, his voice thick with need.

A wicked smile curved her lips. "Patience, young one. We have all night."

They took a short reprieve, their bodies tangled together as they caught their breath. The room was filled with the scent of their passion, a heady aroma that only served to heighten the tension between them.

After a few moments, Alex began to kiss her neck, his hands wandering down her body to play with her breasts. He took a nipple into his mouth, sucking and nipping until it was a hard peak, then moved to the other. Ana moaned, her body responding to his touch despite the intensity of their earlier encounter.

He slid his hand down to her pussy, finding it already wet and swollen. He began to stroke her clit, his movements slow and deliberate. She arched into his touch, her breath hitching as pleasure began to coil in her belly once more. He slid a finger inside her, feeling the slickness of her arousal.

With a growl, he rolled her onto her stomach, his hands spreading her cheeks apart. "You're going to take it all," he murmured, his voice dark with lust. He positioned himself at her entrance, pressing his cock against her ass. She tensed, but he soothed her with gentle kisses along her spine. "Relax, let me in."

He pushed forward, feeling her tightness grip him like a vice. Ana moaned into the pillow, her body stretching to accommodate him. It was a delicious burn, one she hadn't experienced in years. She pushed back against him, urging him deeper.

Alex began to move, his hips slapping against her ass as he fucked her in long, deep strokes. She could feel every inch of him inside her, filling her completely. The sound of their flesh colliding filled the room, a primal symphony that only heightened their desire.

Her moans grew louder, her body moving in tandem with his, meeting each thrust with an eager roll of her hips. He reached under her to play with her clit again, the added sensation sending her spiraling over the edge once more.

This time, as they climaxed together, there was no holding back. Their cries mingled in the night air, a testament to the fierce passion that had ignited between them. As they collapsed onto the bed, their bodies slick with sweat, they knew that their relationship had changed forever.

Experiments

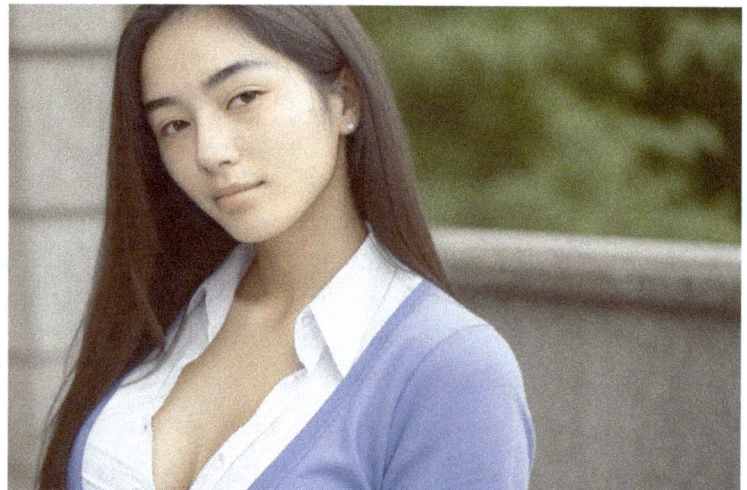

In the quiet, dimly lit library of their university, Tom couldn't help but feel a sense of excitement as he spotted Ava, a shy, brunette beauty, whose almond eyes sparkled like stars in the vast expanse of his fantasies. They had been in the same biology class for two semesters, and every day, she walked in with an air of grace that seemed to silence the whispers of the leaves outside. Her name was Ava, and Tom had been waiting for the perfect moment to make his move. He had noticed her glancing his way during lectures, her cheeks blushing a soft shade of pink, hinting at a curiosity she was too shy to explore. Today, Tom decided, would be the day he unraveled the mystery that was Ava.

Ava was lost in her book, her nose barely touching the pages as she devoured the words. Her soft, full breasts strained against the fabric of her white blouse, and Tom could see the outline of her nipples pushing through, begging for his attention. He took a deep breath, steeling himself for the encounter to come. The anticipation grew as he approached, his heart thumping like a drum in his chest. He sat down at the desk next to her, and the scent of her vanilla perfume filled his nostrils, making his cock stir in his pants.

"Hey, Ava," he whispered, his voice low and seductive. "What are you reading?"

Startled, she looked up, her eyes wide and her cheeks flushing a deeper shade of pink. "Oh, hi, Tom," she replied, her voice a soft melody that made his heart race even faster. "Just catching up on some… biology notes."

Her eyes darted to the textbook on her desk, and Tom knew it was his chance. He leaned in closer, his hand brushing against hers as if by accident. The touch was electric, sending a jolt through her body. She gasped quietly, and he took that as his cue to continue.

Tom's hand began to trace delicate circles around her palm, and

Ava's breath grew shallow. She glanced down at their joined hands, her eyes wide with surprise and desire. He could feel her pulse quicken, and the heat radiating from her body was almost too much to bear. His other hand reached for the hem of her skirt, slowly pulling it upward, revealing her silky smooth thighs. He knew he had to be careful; the last thing he wanted was to scare her away. But the way she leaned into his touch told him she was ready for more.

The tension between them grew as Tom leaned in closer, his lips hovering just a breath away from hers. He could feel her breath, warm and sweet, mingling with his own. "I've wanted this for so long," he murmured, his voice thick with desire. "Do you feel it too?"

Ava's eyes searched his, and she nodded almost imperceptibly. She bit her lower lip, her hand moving to rest on his thigh. The heat from her palm was like a brand, searing through his pants to his hardened cock. He knew she felt it, and the power of knowing he could elicit such a response from her was intoxicating.

Their first kiss was gentle, a soft exploration of each other's lips. It was a promise of things to come, a sweet taste of the passion that simmered beneath their innocent facade. Tom's hand moved from her thigh to her ass, gripping it firmly as he deepened the kiss. Ava moaned into his mouth, and he could feel her body melt into his. His other hand found the clasp of her bra, deftly unhooking it and freeing her breasts. He took one in his hand, marveling at its weight and softness.

EXPERIMENTS

Her nipples were hard and sensitive, and Tom took one between his thumb and forefinger, rolling it gently. Ava gasped, arching her back to push herself closer to him. His mouth moved to capture hers again, their tongues dancing in a silent symphony of desire.

Their kisses grew more frantic as Tom's hand moved between her legs, sliding her panties aside to find her slick, wet entrance. She was already so aroused, and the thought of what he was about to do to her made him ache with need. He stroked her clit gently, feeling it swell beneath his touch. Ava's hips began to rock back and forth, urging him to go faster, harder. She was like a wildflower, desperate for the kiss of the sun.

Tom could no longer resist the siren call of her mouth, and he broke their kiss to trail his lips down her neck, nipping and sucking at the sensitive skin. She moaned, the sound muffled by his shoulder, her eyes fluttering shut as he worked his magic. He felt her hand move to his cock, stroking him through his pants, and the sensation was exquisite. He was so hard it hurt, and he knew he had to have her.

With trembling hands, he unbuckled his belt and unzipped his pants, freeing his erection. It sprang forth, thick and proud, and Ava's eyes widened in a mix of shock and excitement. She took him in her hand, her soft, warm grip making him groan with pleasure. She was tentative at first, her thumb caressing the tip as if it were a precious gem, but as she felt his response, she grew bolder. Her hand began to pump up and down, her movements growing more confident with each stroke.

Tom could feel himself getting closer to the edge, but he didn't want this moment to end so soon. He reached for her hand, stopping her just in time. "Not yet," he whispered, his voice hoarse with need. "Let's find somewhere more... private."

They stumbled out of the library, their breaths coming in gasps, their eyes wild with passion. They found themselves in an empty classroom, the desks and chairs pushed aside to reveal the cold, hard floor. It was the perfect setting for their heated encounter. Ava lay back, her legs spread wide, inviting him in. Tom didn't need another invitation.

He knelt before her, his eyes feasting on her bare pussy. He could see her wetness glistening in the faint light, and he couldn't resist dipping his head to taste her. His tongue slid over her clit, and she cried out, her hips bucking against his mouth. He licked and sucked, his tongue delving into her warm, welcoming vagina. She was like a warm, sweet dessert, and he was a starving man.

Ava's moans grew louder as he worked his tongue, his hands gripping her hips to keep her still. She was so close to the edge, and he could feel her muscles tightening around his tongue. He knew exactly what she needed, and he was more than happy to give it to her. With a final, firm flick of his tongue, she came, her body shaking with the force of her orgasm.

Tom stood up, his cock now slick with her juices. He positioned himself at her entrance, his tip teasing her sensitive folds. Ava looked up at him, her eyes glazed with desire, and whispered, "Take me, Tom."

EXPERIMENTS

And with that, he plunged into her, filling her completely. She was so tight, so warm, so wet. Her walls clamped down around him, and he had to bite back a groan as he felt her pulsate around his cock. He began to thrust, slow and steady, watching as her breasts bounced with each movement.

Their rhythm grew more frantic as they found their pace, their bodies moving in perfect harmony. Ava's hands clawed at his back, her nails digging into his skin as she tried to get closer. He could feel her climbing towards another peak, her breath coming in ragged pants. He reached down to play with her clit again, and she screamed out his name as she came for the second time.

Their climax was explosive, their bodies writhing together as they reached the pinnacle of pleasure. Tom emptied himself into her, feeling her contract around him, her pussy milking him for every drop. They collapsed in a heap, their hearts racing, their bodies sticky with sweat.

For a moment, they lay there, panting and trembling, their eyes locked in a silent promise. They had crossed a line that could never be uncrossed, and Tom knew that from this day forward, Ava would be his in every way that mattered.

Over the following weeks, their secret rendezvous grew more frequent, each encounter a delicious exploration of their deepest desires. They started meeting in various locations across the university, the thrill of being caught only adding to their passion. The risk was intoxicating, and they grew bolder with each meeting.

One afternoon, Ava suggested they try something new, her eyes twinkling with mischief. Tom, eager to please and intrigued by her suggestions, agreed without hesitation. She led him to the biology lab after hours, a place where they knew they'd be undisturbed. The lab coat she had on was the only thing separating him from her naked body, and the thought was driving him wild.

They began to experiment, using various items from the lab to enhance their pleasure. The cold steel of the microscope was a surprising delight against her hot, sensitive skin, making her shiver with anticipation. Tom picked up a glass beaker, filling it with warm water, and he watched as Ava's eyes widened with curiosity. He dipped his fingers into the water, coating them thoroughly before sliding them inside her, feeling the heat of her pussy contrast with the coolness of the liquid.

Her moans grew louder as he inserted another finger, the warmth of her body causing the water to dissipate, creating a sensual, slippery sensation. He watched as her back arched off the desk, her breasts heaving with each ragged breath. Ava was a canvas of ecstasy, and Tom was the artist, eager to paint every inch of her with pleasure.

Their meetings grew more intense, more experimental with each passing day. They tried new positions, explored each other's bodies with an insatiable hunger that seemed to grow with every touch. Ava's innocence was slowly unraveling, revealing a wild, unbridled passion that Tom never knew existed. He found himself falling deeper and deeper under her spell, his every waking moment filled with thoughts of her.

EXPERIMENTS

Their next adventure led them to the university's swimming pool after hours, the water rippling around them like a velvet blanket. Under the dim lights, Tom's eyes devoured Ava's wet, naked body, her skin glistening like a pearl. He slid into the water, his cock hard and ready for her. She straddled him, her legs wrapping around his waist as he filled her once more. The water was a sensual dance partner, caressing their bodies as they moved together.

Their movements were fluid and graceful, their passion mirrored in the waves they created. They kissed deeply, their tongues mimicking the rhythm of their hips, the water acting as a natural lubricant. Ava's breasts bobbed with every stroke, her nipples hard and erect, begging for Tom's mouth. He took one into his mouth, suckling it while his hand found her clit, working it in time with their thrusts.

The water sloshed around them as Ava's orgasm crashed over her, her body convulsing with pleasure. Tom followed suit, his release sending jets of cum into the water around them. They held onto each other, their hearts racing in unison, their breaths mingling as they floated in the afterglow of their love making.

Their affair was a secret garden, lush with the blooms of desire and watered by the sweat of their passionate encounters. Each time they were together, they pushed the boundaries a little further, discovering new ways to pleasure one another. The library was no longer just a place of quiet study, but a sanctuary of lust where they could lose themselves in each other's embrace.

Tom had never felt so alive, so connected to another person. Ava was his muse, his lover, his everything. And as they lay entwined in the water, their bodies still trembling from the aftershocks of ecstasy, he knew that no matter where life took them, this secret they shared would be the most precious memory of their youth.

The TABOOS will continue....

www.ingramcontent.com/pod-product-compliance
Lightning Source LLC
Chambersburg PA
CBHW071053240526
45471CB00015B/1789